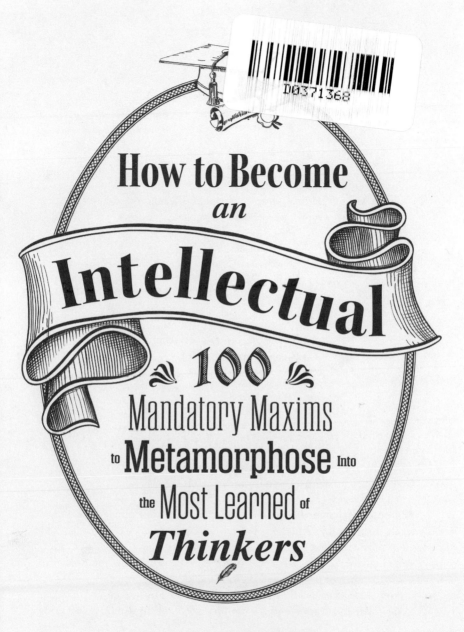

How to Become *an* Intellectual

100 Mandatory Maxims to Metamorphose Into the Most Learned of Thinkers

· NICK KOLAKOWSKI ·

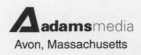

Adamsmedia
Avon, Massachusetts

Dedication

To Mom and Dad—
Smile at the wolf, and the wolf smiles back.

Copyright © 2012 by F+W Media, Inc.
All rights reserved.
This book, or parts thereof, may not be reproduced in any
form without permission from the publisher; exceptions are
made for brief excerpts used in published reviews.

Published by
Adams Media, a division of F+W Media, Inc.
57 Littlefield Street, Avon, MA 02322. U.S.A.
www.adamsmedia.com

ISBN 10: 1-4405-3530-2
ISBN 13: 978-1-4405-3530-7
eISBN 10: 1-4405-3610-4
eISBN 13: 978-1-4405-3610-6

Printed in the United States of America.

10 9 8 7 6 5 4 3 2 1

Library of Congress Cataloging-in-Publication Data
is available from the publisher.

This book is available at quantity discounts for bulk purchases.
For information, please call 1-800-289-0963.

Contents

Introduction

THE ESSAYIST AND CRITIC Christopher Hitchens, writing for the online magazine *Slate*, once described the public intellectual as tasked with introducing "complexity into the argument: the reminder that things are very infrequently as simple as they can be made to seem."

If one were to describe what an intellectual is, that would be a good start: an intellectual is someone who understands and appreciates the complexity of the world, or at least a small corner of it (quantum field theory, the true impact of the Battle of Hastings). I would add that an intellectual also cares passionately about that complexity, which is one reason why fistfights break out in universities over matters people of merely average brainpower would consider petty beyond belief.

But if that's all there is to being an intellectual—thinking complex thoughts and defending said thoughts vigorously—why would you (or anyone) need this book? Why that tongue twister of a subtitle, "100 Mandatory Maxims to Metamorphose Into the Most Learned of Thinkers"?

Intellectuals (or those who aspire to be) sometimes fall into the trap of embracing a tired old stereotype—a caricature, if you will, that results in the world at large thinking of "intellectual" as being roughly equivalent to "elitist," "pompous," and "pretentious."

But there is more to being an intellectual than writing obfuscatory articles for obscure journals and calling one's detractors inflammatory names. Other qualities and characteristics—call them "maxims," because that sounds suitably impressive—define the intellectual: the refusal to let others judge one by one's alma mater (Maxim 2); a commitment to abstain from bullshitting (Maxim 5); the desire to read nearly everything (Maxim 6); the willingness to embrace a few choice eccentricities (Maxim 3) while eschewing others (Maxim 45); the intention of making dates pleasurable instead of competitive (Maxim 62); the dignity to lose debates graciously (Maxim 76); and never succumbing to the temptation to employ Latin in casual conversation (Maxim 80). Most of all, an intellectual is comfortable with saying those three little words that shoot fear into the hearts of the unprepared: "I don't know" (Maxim 17).

In short, an intellectual is the epitome of educated intelligence, coupled with a sensitivity to and appreciation of others—no matter what their IQ.

Acknowledgments

Thanks to the rest of the family, for being there. To Gina, for slow weekend breakfasts; to Erika, for too much to mention; to Nora, for the wit; to Maro, Oliver, Ben, Joe, Patrice, and VJ, for life in the District; to Meredith and Jay, for the manuscript reading, and tales from the belly of the beast; to Yohuru, for the history lessons; to Bradley and Sylvia, for drinks; to Ian L., for the soundtrack; to Ian S., for trips across the third world; to Sara B., for calling out my bullshit; to Sig, for the cigars and advice on Maxim 49; to Nica, for Emily Wells and Roo; to everyone at *McSweeney's*, for finding Nietzsche funny; to Randall, for bringing me to New York; to Rebecca, for the friendship begun on a drifting boat; to Brian, for poker and vodka-fueled bonfires; to Sarah L., for the editing brilliance; to Stephen W., for saving me from the implosion; to Scott F., for making the daily battle against the search algorithms so fun. To Jennifer L., for super-kicking the prose into fine shape.

Most of this book was written to Tom Waits's *Rain Dogs* and The Rolling Stones's *Exile on Main St.*, two of the finest albums ever made.

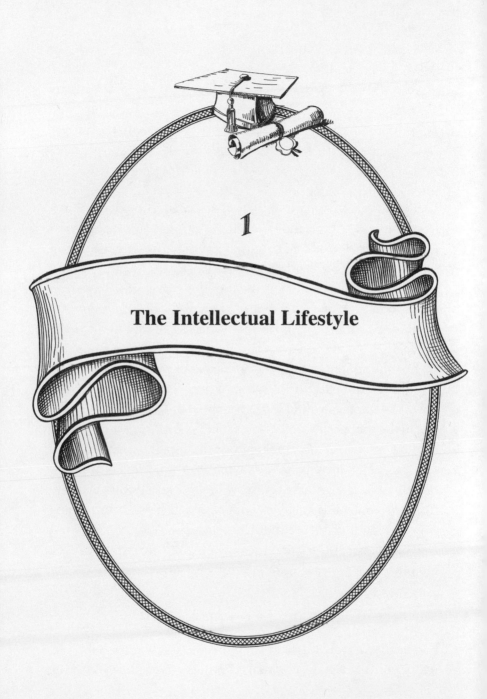

1

The Intellectual Lifestyle

MAXIM 1

CARRY AN INTELLECTUAL BOOK
(AT *ALL* TIMES).

CARRYING A THICK TOME by a well-regarded author is a short-hand method of proclaiming to the world that you are an intellectual. It's a way of signaling that you have an attention span significantly longer than the average Twitter user's and of subtly boasting that you're not intimidated by big words, big ideas, or big books. More than perhaps any other object, a book in hand (or pocket or bag) is the intellectual's calling card; if you're single, it also makes an attractive mating call to other brainiacs.

But your noteworthy book can't serve its purpose if you don't place it prominently on display. Whenever you set your bag down, it behooves you to leave the zipper or flap open, so everyone in the room can admire James Joyce's *Ulysses* or Thomas Pynchon's *Gravity's Rainbow* poking out the top. Alternatively, you can "carelessly" leave your book lying atop your desk at work, to impress colleagues and superiors with your intellectual prowess. Commuting by bus or subway offers similar latitude in flashing your taste in literature, although there's the delicate question of *how* much to tilt the spine to show off the title without being too obvious (answer: around 45 degrees from vertical).

THEORY INTO PRACTICE

For nearly a year, a friend of mine (let's call him Bob) carried around a copy of Herman Melville's *Moby Dick*. With the tenacity of a sailor on a years-long voyage, he plowed through those 700 long-winded pages of watery transcendentalism. Circling the globe in a fishing vessel would have taken less time than it did for him to reach Ahab's climactic battle with the white whale. Yet Bob persevered, taking the book with him everywhere, which suitably impressed everyone who saw it in his hands. Bob's new boss took the book as a sign that his employee was a deep analytical thinker, and doled out the promotions accordingly. Women in grad school would strike up conversations with him at bars. Melville ended up becoming Bob's best wingman ever.

Bob soon realized what was happening, and vowed to make hefting weighty volumes a lifelong habit. Once he finished with Melville, he launched himself into Don DeLillo's *Underworld*, another doorstop thick with theme and characterization. If anyone ever doubted Bob's aspirations to become an intellectual, the sight of those books pretty much ended that.

THE INEVITABLE FOOTNOTE

When random bystanders see you're reading *Ulysses*, they'll often wince in sympathy. Reading Joyce at his most opaque is the intellectual version of cage fighting; the winces serve as our way of comparing the bruises afterward.

If you, however, flash a book as obscure (not to mention incomprehensible) as Philip K. Dick's *Ubik*, random bystanders will not offer the wince of camaraderie. Instead, they will give the furrowed brow of *huh?* That should not dissuade you from reading *Ubik*, but if your main goal in carrying a particular book is to up your intellectual street cred, well, stick with Joyce.

MAXIM 2

EMBRACE YOUR ALMA MATER,
EVEN IF IT'S NOT HARVARD.

A PARTY ATTENDED by intellectuals sometimes descends into the verbal equivalent of a thermonuclear war, one in which the combatants seem determined to transform their rivals into stammering, apologetic poseurs before the hors d'oeuvres are even served. One of the most destructive ICBMs fired during these conflicts is the announcement of one's academic pedigree: where you went to school, what subjects you focused on, which degrees you obtained, and which famous people you studied under.

"Well, when I was at *Harvard*," one scholar might opine, hungering to target that missile straight into his opponent's command-and-control center, "I studied with [insert Nobel Prize winner here], while he was at the absolute height of his powers."

"Well, when I was at *Oxford*," someone else will retort, and the war will escalate from there. The irony is that formal academics aren't the sole (or even the most important) measure of intellectual capacity. Many of history's finest thinkers never attended a prestigious institution, or promptly dropped out to do something else. Bill Gates and Mark Zuckerberg both left Harvard without obtaining a degree, and they're no idiots.

THEORY INTO PRACTICE

As with so many other things in life, a formal education is only worth the amount of effort you put into it. True, a fancy degree can provide the root of a fulfilling, absurdly well-paid career.

But Ivy League graduates also serve as some of this nation's finest baristas. The urge to learn and the discipline to become a true autodidact are what constitute the basis of the intellectual mind.

The next time a missile stamped "Well, when I was in the doctorate program at *Yale*" hurtles toward you, refuse to launch back—especially if you have the credentials to do so. Instead, smile and nod and ask a question about their field of study. Tell yourself that you can learn something new from such a fine mental specimen. And smile. You just won the war.

THE INEVITABLE FOOTNOTE

For very specialized professions, degrees do matter. Let's keep our "nuclear war" metaphor running here, and posit that, in the course of your daily activities, you just happen to stumble across a *real* thermonuclear weapon. If someone steps forward and says, "I can handle this; I have the most advanced degrees in nuclear engineering from MIT and trained in defusing weapons of mass destruction during my stint in the U.S. Air Force," then you step aside and let them debate over whether to cut the blue or red wire. In certain cases, especially in those that involve a chance of death, often the best fallback is to acknowledge a superior brain—and exit the immediate area as quickly as possible.

MAXIM 3

CULTIVATE A FEW CHOICE ECCENTRICITIES.

A VERY THIN LINE EXISTS between insanity and genius. So thin, in fact, that it sometimes disappears completely, and madmen are misidentified as brilliant thinkers, while geniuses are dismissed as lunatics stuffed with an extra helping of crazy.

For every genius mistakenly shipped off to a padded cell, another hundred are dismissed as mere eccentrics, with tics that distinguish them as fish-out-of-water types. Mildly intriguing and definitely harmless, eccentrics include many of history's most famous poets, novelists, mathematicians, theoretical physicists, actors, titans of industry, and half the faculty of the world's universities.

In light of that, cultivating a few eccentricities is practically a requirement for an intellectual. Fortunately, notable role models are everywhere. Despite having parsed some of the universe's most complex secrets, Einstein reportedly never learned to drive, claiming it was too complicated. On top of that, he disdained socks. Legend has it that the French essayist and poet Gérard de Nerval walked around town with a lobster on a leash—which is actually quite inspired, when you consider how few pets also make good eating.

But only a lunatic would embrace eccentricity without a well-thought-out plan.

THEORY INTO PRACTICE

1. Keep it benign: Nobody appreciates a naked gentleman running down the street, smashing windows and screaming about space aliens. The best eccentricities are small and safe. Strange hats and out-of-place accessories (ear horns, etc.) are always favorites, as are unusual hobbies, such as collecting erotic art from pre-Columbian Peru or fashioning household goods out of duct tape. Strange pets are a bit more problematic: a tiger will probably just forego the leash in favor of eating you.

2. Loud and proud: Own your eccentricities with every fiber of your being. An audience will instantly discredit the public performer who displays a hint of uncertainty or doubt. For better or worse, that means any chosen eccentricity needs to be cultivated, practiced, and developed over a long period of time. Being an intellectual requires commitment.

3. Sense of humor: The best eccentricities amuse and delight people. You have to admit, walking a lobster is pretty funny. Well, probably except for the lobster.

THE INEVITABLE FOOTNOTE

More than a few professions and workplaces demand eccentric impulses be kept to a minimum. Hospitals fall into this category: patients tend to become nervous if their neurosurgeon, the same one slated to delicately pick through their parietal lobe, starts walking around with a parrot on her shoulder. Especially a parrot who keeps squawking, "Oops, didn't mean to cut that."

Avoid eccentricities that make it seem like you're trying too hard to be weird. Wearing an antique accessory of some sort, such as a monocle, is often a critical mistake in this category (see Maxim 41: "Decline a pipe or monocle as an accessory"). Remember, you want that eccentricity to seem totally *normal* . . . at least for you.

MAXIM 4

LEARN SOME TRULY ENORMOUS WORDS.

IF ANYTHING MARKS both intellectuals and blowhards who *want* to be intellectuals, it's the ability to deploy multisyllabic words that send everyone scrambling for the nearest dictionary. However, true intellectuals know to deploy these grammatical bunker-busters only when necessary (i.e., when no other word will convey quite the same intended effect) and not to show off the size of their IQ. This is a crucial distinction.

Yet even the most taciturn intellectual can't deny the pleasure of a brobdingnagian word used superlatively. Some of those around you will react with amazement at all those syllables avalanching off your tongue, others with discomfort, or (if their minds are truly blown) perturbation. One hopes none will find your grammatical dexterity annoying enough to take a swing at your head.

THEORY INTO PRACTICE

Many intellectuals-in-training, eager to load their vocabulary with as many ten-dollar words as possible, make the critical mistake of heading right for the dictionary to find appropriately impressive terminology. Once they discover a word that suits their needs, though, they proceed to learn it without a sense of context, and often make grievous (not to mention mockworthy) errors in conversation. "I'm quiescent," they might say. "As in, I totally predicted that would happen." Someone will inevitably point out the correct word is "prescient."

The best way to learn enormous words (and how to use them properly) is to read books that contain such words. Inevitably you stumble across an unknown term, one so splendiferous it leaves you little choice but to hunt down its meaning. By finding these jewels in prose written by someone who knew how to apply them, you instantly gain a sense of their proper use—which means you can wield them more effectively.

At this juncture it really must be reiterated that, when in doubt, use the smallest words possible. That ensures the broadest audience for what you're saying, and prevents you from being grouped with that jackass at the bar who always spouts "antediluvian" in place of "old."

THE INEVITABLE FOOTNOTE

Sometimes only a very specific word will do in a particular situation, with no opportunity to insert a larger or different synonym. Should your sailboat drift off course, forcing you ashore in a mystical land populated by 72-foot-tall people who regard you as a freak of nature, the only possible term for describing your plight is "brobdingnagian," because you've arrived in the land of Brobdingnag, as described in Jonathan Swift's epic *Gulliver's Travels*. You simply can't use a bigger word (no, really, you can't).

MAXIM 5

ABSTAIN FROM BULLSHIT.

IF YOU GO BY THE DICTIONARY DEFINITION, bullshit, meaning something false or exaggerated beyond reasonable proportion, is to be avoided by anyone hoping to be taken seriously by others. But that never stopped anyone from dumping shovelfuls of it into conversation. Who cares about a few pumped-up numbers or highly suspect "quotes" from experts and famous people, so long as it makes you sound smarter?

Other intellectuals care. Despite their emphasis of rationality over emotion, and their willingness to talk through issues rather than resort to fists, intellectuals tend to be highly competitive animals (anyone who's ever attended a literary reading with multiple authors vying for the audience's attention, or a faculty lounge down to its last half-pot of coffee, will know what I mean). Attempt to deploy bullshit within their earshot, and they will move to pick apart your talk, loudly, making sure everyone knows they were smart enough to recognize you as a poseur.

Or, even worse, they'll bide their time and wait until you leave the room, then perform the same public evisceration without giving you a chance to defend yourself. An intellectual get-together can rival the Serengeti in a drought for sheer viciousness.

THEORY INTO PRACTICE

Most bullshitters are caught when they start jabbering about topics well beyond their knowledge zone. You can entertain a party with an impressive-sounding monologue about the origins of the universe, based only on details from a half-remembered newspaper article—until an actual physicist steps forward to offer a correction that splatters your bullshit story with the force of a sledgehammer hitting a wedding cake. Your reputation will only recover slowly from that incident.

If you need a role model for this maxim, look to Thomas Jefferson, who once said: "He who permits himself to tell a lie once, finds it much easier to do it a second and third time, till at length it becomes habitual." To succeed in bullshit once is temptation to try it again. Overstretch, and sooner or later another scholarly type might take the opportunity to finish you off in front of a crowd.

THE INEVITABLE FOOTNOTE

In certain situations, a sprinkle of bullshit can spare you considerable embarrassment.

"A giant deer sprinted right into our headlights. I had to stop and wait for it to pass. It didn't seem worth wrecking my car hood just to get some venison," you tell the attendees at your book reading or speech. They will probably laugh. It sounds plausible. And it certainly beats admitting that you managed to accidentally lock yourself in a gas-station bathroom for thirty minutes.

MAXIM 6

READ AND COMPREHEND
(NEARLY) EVERYTHING.

THE TRUE INTELLECTUAL is a glutton for reading material. Magazines and scholarly journals, biographies and other nonfiction, novels and short stories, poetry and street posters: all beg for attention and study. Through reading we absorb some of the richest ideas floating through the collective unconsciousness, the ones too subtle and complex for expression in a two-hour movie or pithy sound bite. These ideas, in turn, solidify the foundation on which the intellectual builds his or her own palace of knowledge. There's a reason scholars assemble expansive libraries, and it's not because books make dynamite wall furnishings.

Some concepts absorbed through reading are easy to comprehend. Who doesn't get the moral in Aesop's fable of the tortoise and the hare, or understand why Hamlet wants to stab his father's killer? Still other texts prove far more difficult to digest, especially "experimental" ones along the lines of Joyce's *Finnegans Wake* (with its narrative use of idioglossia, which just became your dictionary word of the day) or Neal Stephenson's *Anathem* (a sprawling novel, its difficulty trebled by virtue of being written in a fictional dialect of English).

The intellectual should make an effort to comprehend the themes and plots of the more difficult texts, and not only because other intellectuals frequently cite such works as their "favorites." Absorbing them adds the highest-quality material to the intellectual's knowledge base, in turn enriching his or her own thoughts. Plus it gives you something new to brag about at parties.

THEORY INTO PRACTICE

The intellectual at a loss for reading matter should consider the Modern Library's 100 Best Novels (the list, including Fitzgerald's *The Great Gatsby* and Nabokov's *Lolita*, is available at *www.modernlibrary.com*), as well as recommendations from friends with trusted taste.

Reading is one thing, but comprehension is quite another. The first time I picked up Dante's *Inferno* (the Robert Pinsky translation), it quickly became my Battle of the Somme, a line-by-line grind through the rhetorical mud in search of understanding: too many references to obscure Italian counts, Renaissance assassinations, monsters from antiquity. For many of history's greatest works that prove difficult, publishers offer an "annotated edition" complete with copious notes and explanations. Find it.

With the classics under their belt, the reader will inevitably gravitate to material that sparks their emotions: if horror's your thing, start with Edgar Allan Poe and read straight through to Peter Straub. If you've always been interested in the American Civil War, endless library bookshelves groan with fiction and nonfiction texts for you to peruse at your leisure—although if you want an exemplary volume in that category, seek out John Keegan's *The American Civil War: A Military History*.

Most constant readers find a balance between the complex "deep" stuff (i.e., Nabokov, weighty biographies of famous historical figures) lightened with servings of frothy popular literature and nonfiction.

THE INEVITABLE FOOTNOTE

A minister of my acquaintance balances open books on the steering wheel while he drives, trusting in a kind and loving universe to spare him from accident while absorbed in a good book (or, often, *the* good book). This is not recommended. Limit your reading to safe moments.

MAXIM 7

GIVE YOUR SIGNATURE
SOME CHARACTER.

BACK WHEN COMPOSING a multipage letter was humanity's only form of long-distance communication, as opposed to tapping out "OMG LMAO" on their phones, people made it a point to develop their handwriting, and thought long and deep about the style of their signatures. The advent of keyboards and screens has made longhand a lost art. And signatures? John Hancock, he of arguably the most notable old-school signature ever scratched on paper, would have an aneurism if he saw the messy scrawl that passed for most people's autographs on contracts and checks.

John Hancock belonged to the previous generations who believed in a signature's ability to suggest, in a few swoops of ink, the writer's refinement. His name on the Declaration of Independence includes all manner of loops and swirls and decorative underscoring, large enough (legend has it) for King George III to read without his spectacles. But those eleven letters are more than a middle finger to a despot: they convey Hancock's education, sense of taste, and bold personality. In the era before telephones and e-mail, thinkers from all walks of life—politicians like Hancock and the other Founding Fathers, writers, philosophers—meant their signatures as a quick and not-so-subtle hint of their enormous intellect. That mode of thinking has largely disappeared over the past few decades, and that's a shame—no, "tragedy" is probably a better term for it. Kids these days have no respect for the old ways of doing things. Now get off my lawn.

THEORY INTO PRACTICE

Grade school was the last time most people paid attention to their signatures, and that was under penalty of failing Handwriting. You wouldn't trust a fourth grader behind the wheel of a truck, and yet you've let your inner elementary-school student control one of the main ways in which you're perceived by the world at large.

Take out a piece of blank paper. Write your signature at a normal (i.e., comfortable) speed. Do you like how it looks? Or would you prefer it convey a little more stateliness, maybe with a few swirls? Or perhaps your tastes veer more to the eccentric, and you feel the ideal signature demands a jagged "lightning bolt" sort of look.

Your next step involves experimenting with letters and forms— taking care to ensure that, above all, your signature is legible. It will take some time before you settle on something you like: behind every John Hancock is a mountain of balled-up paper.

Then practice, until you replicate it the same way every time.

THE INEVITABLE FOOTNOTE

Many years ago, I worked for a university press where an editor made a point to sign every rejection letter himself. Considering the number of unsolicited submissions that poured into the mailroom every morning (we demanded that prospective authors query via snail-mail, perhaps out of the misguided idea that it would some-how slacken that unending tide), this meant an incredible number of signatures needed dispensing by closing time.

Under the pressure of that time-crunch, the editor's signature, once an elaborate thing of beauty, had flattened into a straight line with a meaningless little bump in the middle. It was as sad as a flat-lining EKG, but in the name of speed it did the job. Still, if you have a lot of papers to sign in a very limited amount of time and want to send out each one with your distinctive autograph, consider purchasing a signature stamp.

MAXIM 8

NEVER UTTER THESE FIVE PHRASES.

The intellectual will speak millions of words in a lifetime. From this tumult of noise emerge brilliant theories, biting witticisms, satisfying insults, elusive metaphors, or a confused plea for help when confronted with fixing a leaky sink faucet.

Human language is a wonderful tool—but also one that, like a greased chainsaw, can bounce back to do some harm if you're not careful. For the intellectual, the danger of the *mal mot* is twofold. Not only do you need to beware of the usual foot-in-mouth phrases ("Why yes, that dress does make you look fat"), but a host of others that can crumble your carefully built façade as a thinking person's thinking person. Therefore, you must at all costs avoid uttering certain inanities.

THEORY INTO PRACTICE

These verbal landmines include:

1. "I don't read fiction." If I had a dollar for each time I've heard this one uttered at an "intellectual" gathering, I could afford to buy a Porsche for every day of the week. People often use this line out of a need to appear serious, as if only reading nonfiction somehow elevates them above life's frivolities (never mind that fiction constitutes a significant portion of every culture's DNA). Plus, you know they're hiding a well-thumbed copy of a Dan Brown novel on their bookshelf at home, the same way someone on a diet keeps a cupcake in the back of the fridge.

2. "Someday I'm becoming a hermit." The fantasy of many a stressed-out intellectual: take refuge in a rustic cabin, far away from the not-so-civilized world, and spend your days in peaceful contemplation. Except everybody knows you'll never do it, mostly because the local Thai place refuses to deliver to mountain hideaways. To mutter that you're interested in the hermit lifestyle is just an indicator to anyone within earshot that you're barely in control of your frenetic existence. And the intellectual always needs to maintain the illusion of control.

3. "I'm always right." Gripped by some toxic combination of hubris and alcohol, the intellectual will declare he's incapable of being wrong. Which is just wrong, because everybody is wrong on occasion. Spout that phrase too many times, and prepare for the inevitable accusations of arrogance and conceitedness.

4. "I'm not talking about this anymore." Usually offered in a desperate bid to terminate an endless debate over . . . well, um, something. Wait, how did this conversation start? Never mind. Keep talking: with an intellectual, the discussion is only over when one side of the debate passes out at the table.

5. "That's just stupid." Yes, everyone will let slip a foolish phrase on occasion. Yes, they say things based on misinformation—remember, at one point Europeans thought the world was flat as a pancake. If you take issue with another point of view, it's often better for everyone involved if you couch your disagreement in kind and reasonable terms, in order to prevent hurt feelings and needless fights. Especially if they're a prizefighter with a nasty left. And they believe the world is flat.

THE INEVITABLE FOOTNOTE

Whatever I say, I'm always right. And you're an idiot. That's why I'm becoming a hermit and bringing no novels with me. End of discussion.

MAXIM 9

TELL JOKES ONLY 0.05 PERCENT OF PEOPLE WILL UNDERSTAND.

Understanding an in-joke is the surest sign that you're a member of an exclusive club. This holds doubly true for intellectuals, who consider it high art to take bits of knowledge and bend them into puns. Well, *most* intellectuals: some treat every aspect of their work with a monkish seriousness, busting out the Fists of Fury—or at least the Stern Look of Disappointment—if you make any attempt to see the humor in their field. That sternness is worthy of some respect, so long as the field in question doesn't involve an intensive, academic analysis of the movies of Kevin Smith.

For everybody else, a good joke acts as a secret double-handshake, revealing you as a member of good standing among the knowledge-centric. The more esoteric the humor, the higher your implied level of knowledge. At the same time, you need to guarantee that your wit stays accessible: a joke so inscrutable it can only be deciphered by three geniuses is pretty much pointless, unless you deploy it with the express purpose of driving a dinner party into awkward silence.

THEORY INTO PRACTICE

If your audience is philosophy majors, try this one:

"Descartes walks into a bar. The bartender says to him, 'Do you want a beer?' Descartes looks him in the eye and says, 'I think not,' and promptly disappears like he never existed."

If they're chemists, try this one:

"What element is the biggest drag at the party? Bohrium! Get it?"

I'm here all week, folks, try the veal.

A laugh, a smile: that's all you need to know you've found some new members of your particular club.

THE INEVITABLE FOOTNOTE

There are jokes with surefire appeal to intellectuals of a particular field, and those that confuse anyone and everyone. When in doubt, choose the quips and stories that play well with a broader audience. "There are three kinds of people: those who understand math, and those who don't" is a witticism that falls into that category.

MAXIM 10

CHOOSE YOUR INTELLECTUAL ROLE MODEL.

EVERYBODY NEEDS A ROLE MODEL. Your nephew loves baseball, wants to be a major-league player when he grows up, and will probably nurture that dream until another little punk tells him that few human beings can hit a ball more than 450 feet without a little help from steroids. Intellectual role models are much easier to embrace, if only because the physical standards are so much lower. Nobody cares if a famous theorist or world-class poet lived on a gallon of coffee and two packs of unfiltered cigarettes a day, because what ultimately matters is the results of their thinking. For aspiring intellectuals, a role model proves that all the pondering and toil can (against all odds) end in recognition, validation, and triumph.

THEORY INTO PRACTICE

Choosing a specific role model is largely dependent on your personal interests; but all role models, no matter what the nature of their work, share one common trait: their example encourages those who come after them to reach further. The quote, "If I have seen further it is by standing on the shoulders of giants" is attributed to Sir Isaac Newton, who subsequently became a giant to two centuries' worth of physicists. In the work of our role models, we find the hope that we can someday achieve on a similar level.

Literature: If you're a literary-minded intellectual, you can have your pick of role models. Dante and Shakespeare wrote verse that has withstood time's every test. Hemingway's stripped-down style proves an irresistible temptation to legions of budding writers, as does Hunter S. Thompson's gonzo prose. Joyce Carol Oates offers a template for anyone who aspires to be ultra-prolific and endlessly versatile.

Science: Marie Curie was the first woman to win a Nobel Prize, and the first person to win two, for her work in physics and chemistry. Galileo pushed his theory of the earth rotating the sun, despite the opposition of the authorities. Charles Darwin, Alan Turing, and Albert Einstein advocated groundbreaking theories despite considerable personal hardship and, often, doubts from their colleagues. This perseverance in the face of extreme adversity elevates them as role models for any scientist toiling to peek into the universe's clockwork.

Business: Henry Ford developed the manufacturing assembly line for his automobiles, birthing the modern factory. Apple CEO Steve Jobs grew his company from the edge of insolvency to one of the largest in the world. Both executives stand as examples of how innovation can create a business juggernaut.

Art: Sculptors might look up to Alexander Calder, whose airy "mobiles" redefined sculpture; painters to Georgia O'Keeffe, and her still-lifes that remain synonymous with the American West, or to Pablo Picasso and his groundbreaking work in Cubism and other genres; photographers to Diane Arbus or Man Ray, who shot iconic photographs and, in the latter case, helped develop techniques such as photograms; animators to John Lasseter, whose Pixar films demonstrate how computer animation can be used in service of great stories.

History and Politics: History belongs to the victors, according to the old saying—but it's the job of historians and political analysts to frame the past in a way that gives people some insight into the present. Howard Zinn belongs on that list of notable historians, thanks to his *A People's History of the United States* and its alternative view to what you were taught in high school. Adam Smith (*The Wealth of Nations*) and Alexis de Tocqueville (*Democracy in America*) composed works about the economy and the early United States, respectively, that more than two hundred years later are still cited by historians as insightful texts.

THE INEVITABLE FOOTNOTE

You can debate endlessly whether certain famous figures' not-so-stellar personal lives and beliefs disqualify them from serving as role models. Some intellectual titans have been incredible thinkers but—let's not mince words about this—abhorrent human beings. Pablo Picasso left stories of infidelity and abuse in his wake. Steve Jobs famously ripped into anyone he perceived as an idiot. Whether that sort of behavior bars someone from becoming your figurehead is a personal choice; if you're public about adulating them, be prepared to deal with the inevitable questions about their biography's unsavory aspects.

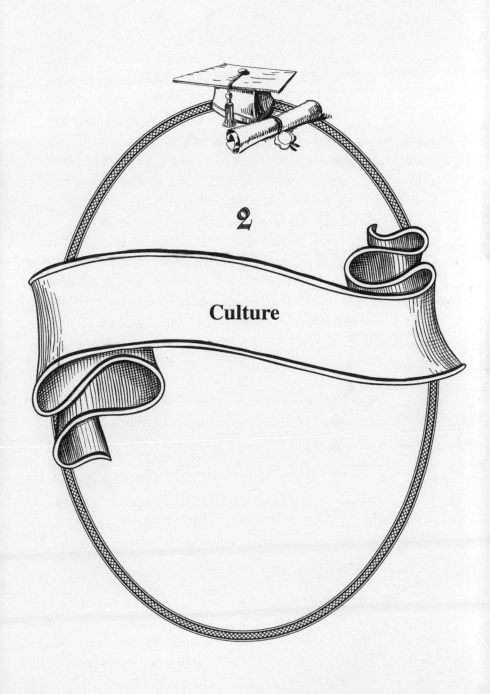

2

Culture

MAXIM 11

ENJOY POPULAR CULTURE.

PEOPLE WHO WANT others to respect their intellectual horse-power will sometimes use pop culture as a piñata. They make a show of disdaining summer blockbusters, turn their noses at books that make the bestseller list, and absolutely abhor, with a passion usually reserved for those fighting a decades-long civil war, any sonic confectionary that tops the music charts. At the same time, they affect an intense enjoyment of life's higher-minded offerings. "I took Baudrillard's *Simulacra and Simulation* to the beach with me last weekend," one such blowhard might say. "I'm really enjoying its take on cultural materialism."

This attitude does not make you an intellectual so much as a solid contender for the World's Most Pretentious Jackass Award.

"Popular" culture and "high" culture have always blended together. The Elizabethan playwrights, endlessly dissected by English departments worldwide, including Shakespeare, wrote primarily for the popular audience. History's most influential directors, such as Stanley Kubrick and Alfred Hitchcock, crafted big movies for mass consumption. Raymond Chandler, in his acclaimed novel *The Big Sleep*, used the elements of pulp fiction to create literature.

THEORY INTO PRACTICE

None of this means you need to enjoy every movie in which Bruce Willis in a semi-trailer plays chicken with a low-flying F-35, or to force-feed yourself a four-hundred-page novel about vampires in love. Nonetheless, making a point to absorb and enjoy pop culture accomplishes two ends:

1. It Makes You Approachable: People seek common ground with others, often by asking whether they've seen a particular movie or television show, or read a certain book. A discussion about any of those is an easy way to kick off a conversation and ease into a relationship.

2. It Gives You More Material: Popular culture bleeds into high culture, and vice versa. Jay-Z name-drops Plato and Socrates in "No Church in the Wild." The artist Damien Hirst creates the album cover for the Red Hot Chili Peppers' *I'm with You*. Once you've exhausted high culture as a source for metaphors, theories, and similes, popular culture presents a whole new well of material for your next intellectual brawl.

Many elements of pop culture are the mental equivalent of a jumbo bag of potato chips, exciting to your brain's pleasure centers but utterly devoid of intellectual nutrition. But who cares, in moderation? I know a MacArthur Genius with a not-so-secret love for pro wrestling.

THE INEVITABLE FOOTNOTE

Refrain from having an opinion on pop culture you haven't read, seen, or heard (see Maxim 5: "Abstain from bullshit"). People are passionate about their movies and music, and will riddle you with rhetorical holes if you try to argue a point of view you hijacked from the reviews section of the local paper. "His lyrics suck," you might say, despite having never heard a single profanity-laden couplet from that particular artist. "Which lyrics do you mean?" your friend will shoot back. You will have no reply. And thereafter you look like an idiot, not an intellectual.

KNOW YOUR MANET FROM YOUR MONET.

From Vincent van Gogh's sunflowers to that framed piece of crap hanging in your dentist's office, humankind has produced a lot of famous and not-so-famous paintings. There is therefore little shame in viewing an unfamiliar work of art and saying, "I have no idea who painted that," rather than make an uneducated guess (see Maxim 17: "Become comfortable with saying, 'I don't know.'"). The penalty for the latter is severe: stepping in front of a Gauguin classic and telling anyone within earshot, "Wow, Klimt really did know how to wield a brush, didn't he?" will result in your permanent ban from any self-respecting museum. Actually, I'm kidding about that last part. But misnaming an artist still won't do wonders for your budding intellectual reputation.

THEORY INTO PRACTICE

Reading up on history's artistic movements will familiarize you with the masterpieces. In the meantime, here are some common trouble spots when it comes to keeping your Manets and Masaccios straight:

The Italian Renaissance: How many brilliant artists did the Italian Renaissance produce? Leonardo da Vinci painted the *Mona Lisa*, Michelangelo set the standard for housepainters everywhere with the ceiling of the Sistine Chapel, Botticelli gave the world his *Venus*, and the works of Raphael and Masaccio spawned legions of frustrated imitators. With so much iconic art created in a few decades' time, it can prove difficult to keep track of every work. Even so, don't slip up and say that Botticelli gave the *Mona Lisa* her smile. Instead, spend some time familiarizing yourself with the greats from this era.

Manet and Monet: Édouard Manet and Claude Monet, pivotal figures of French Impressionism, not only lived during the same time period (Manet was born in 1832, Monet in 1840) but also knew each other. (Generations of art professors have tortured their students with "Was this painted by Manet or Monet?" quizzes.)

While the two artists shared some stylistic tendencies, they weren't exactly the Siamese twins of the Impressionist movement. Manet preferred painting portraits, often placing his subjects within a bustling scene, as with *A Bar at the Folies-Bergère* (exhibited at the 1882 Paris Salon). Monet was more of a landscape painter, intent on reducing fields and water lilies and haystacks to essences of color—his *The Water-Lily Pond*, from 1899, is a prime example of this.

Got that? Good, because there might be a quiz later.

Cubism: Early in the twentieth century, a handful of artists found themselves bored by painting and sculpting reality. They began deconstructing traditional forms, transforming objects and people alike into visual blizzards of angles and panes and color. Some of the world's most notable painters embraced this new avantgarde movement, from Georges Braque and Pablo Picasso to Marcel Duchamp and Jean Metzinger. But show someone a Cubist image, and they will likely revert to the standard answer for any innovative painting: "Um, Picasso?" Nope. The Cubists were more than Pablo.

Unfortunately, it can prove difficult to distinguish Cubists based on their style. Picasso's *Still Life with a Bottle of Rum* (1911) is unnervingly similar in color and brushstroke to Braque's *Candlestick and Playing Cards on a Table* (1910), for instance. Better to memorize individual works than risk confusing painters.

Francis Bacon and Lucian Freud: Both painters, enormously influential on the British art scene following World War II, offered up portraits of humanity as a fleshy and vital thing. Bacon's paintings, at first glance, are saturated with a greater darkness, an emphasis on people as flawed meat. Freud's portraits likewise displayed people at their most flawed and sinewy, but with warmer colors, and less infused with an overwhelming sense of doom.

THE INEVITABLE FOOTNOTE

In a crowded gallery, confusing a painter out loud could draw the attention of a nearby art professor or curator, who, if you're lucky, will offer a quick (and illuminating) lecture. Actually, chances of that are slim, so you're better off taking one of those guided tours offered by most museums.

KNOW THE BASICS OF CHESS.

THE GAME OF CHESS takes a lifetime to master and roughly fifteen minutes to kick your ass. Your sixteen pieces—more on what they do in a minute—move across the chessboard's sixty-four squares in a dizzying variety of ways. (If you're interested in exactly how many, take a moment and look up the "Shannon number," which is the estimated lower bound for the total number of legal chess moves. It's, uh, not small.) Chess masters think dozens of potential moves ahead, formulating strategy to not only parry your next attack but the attack after that and the attack after that. Meanwhile you sit there and sweat, faint smoke dribbling from your ears as your brain grinds toward computational meltdown, anxious only to avoid a truly humiliating defeat.

The chessboard has long served as the intellectual's substitute for heading to war. Indeed, chess offers a key advantage over real-world combat: the thrill of victory, with none of the dirt, sweat, blood, smoke, pain, or sleeping in the mud. You can sip tea or take a break midway through the battle, should you choose.

Chess also exists as the purest form of intellectual competition this side of a university debate. Head to any major urban park on a sunny afternoon and find the chess hustlers on the benches, decimating all challengers willing to slap down a five-dollar bill. No matter what your profession or salary, a game or two will expose your true aptitude for strategy and abstract thinking. Which is why, if you move in intellectual circles, sooner or later you could find yourself on the other side of the checkered board from an opponent. Be prepared.

THEORY INTO PRACTICE

By manipulating various pieces—pawns, rooks (castles), knights, a queen, and a king, each of which can move only in specified patterns—the players try to anticipate and counter each other's strategy. (Numerous books offer a more intensive breakdown of the game's rules, including champion Bobby Fischer's *Bobby Fischer Teaches Chess* and Patrick Wolff's *The Complete Idiot's Guide to Chess*.)

The ultimate goal is to place your opponent's king in checkmate, preventing it from moving in any direction without running into another piece's attack radius. For most players, this means decimating their opponent's pieces until the king is left isolated.

In order to reach that point, a game usually progresses in three stages:

1. Opening: Central to a successful set of opening moves is controlling the middle of the board, and protecting your king from any stupid mistakes.

2. Middle Game: The messy part, involving strategies and counter-strategies.

3. Endgame: The grand finale, in which the few surviving pieces jockey for position. The king is more exposed and at risk.

No matter how savvy your skills, you will face eventual defeat. Even Garry Kasparov, a chess grandmaster of such intimidating skill his mere glance could make a lesser chess player break down and weep, lost to a glorified toaster named Deep Blue. The key is to lose with grace (see Maxim 76 if you need assistance with this). Or as Benjamin Franklin wrote in 1779, as part of *The Morals of Chess*: "If the game is not to be played rigorously . . . then moderate your desire of victory over your adversary, and be pleased with one over yourself." But you still owe that chess hustler his five bucks.

THE INEVITABLE FOOTNOTE

There are none. To decline a game of chess with another intellectual is tantamount to a nineteenth-century warrior-poet backing down from a battle or duel. At least with chess, you can lose and survive to learn from the experience.

MAXIM 14

PLAY AT LEAST ONE
CLASSICAL INSTRUMENT.

ONCE UPON A TIME, mastery of a musical instrument was considered one of the foundations of a well-rounded education, along with the ability to think analytically and, depending on the society and time in question, fight on horseback (the latter's probably unnecessary in a modern-day context, although it would make boardroom meetings a lot less boring). That's all mostly in the past, because now "well-rounded education" is often synonymous with "fill out the right bubbles on a standardized test." Still, it means people will be that much more mind-blowingly impressed when you pick up a violin and whip out, seemingly from nowhere, a decent Mendelssohn concerto.

Actually learning to play a classical instrument is in many ways the intellectual equivalent of training to become a Navy SEAL: it involves massive amounts of concentration and skill, endurance against incredible odds, and a diehard willingness to repeat the same actions over and over until they become gut instinct—but hopefully requires a lot less blood and gunfire.

THEORY INTO PRACTICE

Choose Your Weapon, er, Instrument: If you've long harbored fantasies of becoming the next Frederic Chopin (one of the greatest maestros of the piano) or Joshua Bell (one of the best modern violinists), it's always a good time to give the musical life a real-life try. First rule: proceed slowly. Listen to as much classical music as you can, to hear which instrument plays your heartstrings. Ask musician friends for their advice. Finally, rent an instrument and take it for a long test run.

Learn to read sheet music: You can play an instrument without ever learning how to read sheet music (some of history's greatest musicians were illiterate in this way), but training yourself to read those notes and little squiggles gives you the ability to play classical music you've never heard before. Plus it saves you time learning new songs, should the urge seize you to serenade your upcoming party with a little Mozart.

Practice: It won't get you to Carnegie Hall by next week, but it will ensure that whatever you play won't sound like a panicked coyote locked in a music store. Recognize that every instrument has its quirks, which take some time to recognize. And most of all, follow that music-instructor cliché about playing with passion—otherwise, your music will sound rote.

THE INEVITABLE FOOTNOTE

Guitars are cool. Thanks to generations of flaxen-haired rock gods, a sleek six-stringer vibrates with sex appeal. Too bad the modern guitar isn't really a factor in many "classical" compositions: therefore, if you're intent on playing a classical instrument, there's no wiggle room for a Stratocaster. Besides, carrying a guitar is more liable to make people think you're trying out for an AC/DC cover band, as opposed to studying music theory in the footsteps of the masters. If you want to play a stringed instrument, pick the lute.

UNDERSTAND OPERA,
EVEN IF YOU NEVER ENJOY IT.

THE HISTORY OF OPERA begins some four hundred years ago in Italy, when singing became an integral part of stage performance. By the latter half of the eighteenth century, as Wolfgang Amadeus Mozart sat down to pen *The Magic Flute* and other immortal operas, the setting of a dramatic text to music had evolved in elaborate, expressive ways. In the modern era, musicians such as Philip Glass have continued to push opera in new directions. Other types of performance wax and wane in popularity, and yet opera houses worldwide fill with aficionados year after year.

Then you have the anti-aficionados, who would prefer a double root canal from a dentist with the shakes than endure three hours of opera. They would likely agree with the composer Claude Debussy, who once opined, "In opera, there is always too much singing." In their minds, the performances are stuffy and incomprehensible, filled with singers bellowing in a strange tongue.

You don't have to enjoy the music, but given all that history—not to mention opera's long association with the cerebral set—it's probably worth understanding *why* so many people dress their best and head out to hear the fat lady sing.

Because many operas are sung in languages other than English, you may not immediately realize that the plots are rather straightforward and easy to understand. Take Mozart's comedy *The Marriage of Figaro*: Figaro and Susanna, two servants to a thoroughly lecherous count, try to fend off their boss long enough to actually marry each other.

Listening to the music, and knowing some of the fundamentals behind it, can boost your appreciation of opera.

THEORY INTO PRACTICE

Think of opera as a cold bath: you need to ease yourself into it very slowly. The dipping-the-toe part involves actually listening to opera. Experts recommend starting with composers such as Mozart or Verdi, who were popular in their day for entertaining, action-packed works. You can afford to wait a little bit before testing your appetite for the more avant-garde composers and their five-hour epics of sonic weirdness.

But listening to disembodied music through a set of tinny speakers will carry you only so far. The next step is to attend an opera in person. Tickets can be expensive, and opera houses generally forbid casual wear: the form started as entertainment for royals and the upper crust, which in turn influenced the dress code forever afterward. Leave the AC/DC T-shirt and the shorts at home. Seeing an opera as the original composer intended, complete with costumes and singers trembling the air with their voices, will make the stuffy clothing worth it.

If you live far from the madding crowds, you may not be able to see an opera in person, but many movie theaters screen live performances from the Met—not quite the same thing as being there, but close.

THE INEVITABLE FOOTNOTE

Some operas are easier to absorb than others. Even though Francis Ford Coppola made Richard Wagner's *Ride of the Valkyries* familiar to millions of people by using it in a key scene in *Apocalypse Now*, Wagner isn't your best bet if you're just starting out. His Ring Cycle operas, for instance, each feature several hours of intense, brass-heavy music, more than capable of wearing down all but the hardiest neophytes. If you're interested in exploring opera, start with shorter and more melodic operas by Mozart and Verdi.

MAXIM 16

QUOTE SHAKESPEARE SPARINGLY.

QUOTING WILLIAM SHAKESPEARE is a little like breathing: every living person does it. "He's dead as a doornail," your room-mate will say as she flips through the newspaper obits, never realizing she's just quoted part of a couplet from *Henry VI*. Or take another well-worn phrase, "Let's give the devil his due": it appears in *Henry IV*. (Ol' Billy did love writing about royals.)

Then come the billion lines instantly recognizable as Shake-speare. Case in point: "To be, or not to be." Thanks to the enormous number of movies, television shows, cartoons, comic strips, and probably cereal boxes that have riffed off that line over the years, even if you slept through high school English, you know it comes from *Hamlet*.

The good thing about quoting Shakespeare is that it usually sounds so *perfect* that whoever is arguing with you is suddenly less inclined to disagree with whatever point or idea you're using the quote to enforce—whether or not they know the quote came from the Bard's pen. (There's a reason why the man's works have endured for so long.) The bad thing about quoting Shakespeare is that everybody's been doing it for hundreds of years, meaning that many of the best phrases are overused. That's right: they're trite, and being trite is anathema to an intellectual.

Does that mean you should banish Shakespeare, *King Lear*-style, from your arsenal of everyday quotes? Absolutely not. Simply keep in mind that a little bit of him goes a very, very long way.

THEORY INTO PRACTICE

Shakespeare was just one of many Elizabethan playwrights scribbling out a living on tales of irate royals turning each other into human pincushions. If you want a quote or speech with some of that late-sixteenth-century flavor, other options abound: Christopher Marlowe was another scribbler of some of the finest blank verse ever committed to parchment; his "Thou hast committed—/ Fornication: but that was in another country; And besides, the wench is dead" says as much about true love as anything in Shakespeare's poetry. Those looking for another quotable notable can seek out Sir Walter Raleigh, who gave the world a decent phrase or two.

Should you want to diversify even further (yes, you do), there exist centuries of quotes from virtually every imminent brain to ever wield a pen: Arthur Miller, Simone de Beauvoir, Norman Mailer, Teddy Roosevelt, and Nikolai Gogol constitute a mere fraction of the writers who sweated, bled, agonized, and tortured themselves over a sentence in order to provide you, years later, with the ideal epigraph for your PowerPoint presentation opener.

THE INEVITABLE FOOTNOTE

Shakespeare will always offer an ideal fallback for quotes, particularly if (a) you really want to quote Shakespeare, second-guessing by other intellectuals be damned, or (b) you want to drop a phrase or speech familiar to everyone in the room. With one exception: never, ever employ the phrase "Something's rotten in the state of Denmark" (yes, *Hamlet* again) to describe something trite like a lack of coffee in the house; a dim buzzing sound will fill the world, as an irate Billy spins in his grave fast enough to shoot him straight to the Earth's molten core.

MAXIM 17

BECOME COMFORTABLE WITH SAYING,
"I DON'T KNOW."

SOME PEOPLE HAVE A HARD TIME admitting they don't know everything. Ask a question outside their knowledge safety-zone, and instead of outright confessing they have no idea, they invent an answer, they demand clarification of the question, they equivocate, they hem, they haw. But admit the answer isn't imprinted on their gray matter? They'd rather be clubbed like a baby seal.

The stalling fools nobody. It only attracts a look of deep pity from the listener. There is simply no reason to prolong that agony when your flummoxed self can simply voice those three magic words: "I don't know."

THEORY INTO PRACTICE

Saying, "I don't know" is an incredible challenge for those who previously spent years self-defining by their sheer breadth of knowledge.

The time has come (the walrus said) to internalize that a gap in your knowledge is not a sign of failure as an intellectual. Nothing could be further from the truth. If everybody knew everything, there would be little need for intellectual pursuits, and thus no reason for rolling out of bed in the morning. That's the real explanation for why physicists have never offered a Theory of Everything: if they did, their sole task in life would become sending each other dirty jokes coded inside equations.

Having a natural sense of curiosity about the unknown is one of the great joys in life, and it starts with a simple phrase.

Say it with me now. Usher everyone else from the room and lock the door, if that helps. Find a mirror and enunciate very clearly: "I. Don't. Know."

That felt liberating, didn't it? If you didn't before, try it now in the presence of actual people.

THE INEVITABLE FOOTNOTE

Certain things in life need a definitive answer, one way or another. "Did you turn the water off?" is not something to which you reply, "I don't know," at least if you want the house to remain intact.

Similarly, when asked to perform basic tasks—i.e., changing a tire, or doing a load of laundry—"I don't know" is rarely the right response. You might not always know whether William Faulkner won the Nobel Prize for Literature (answer: yes) or the capital of Paraguay (Asunción, a lovely town), and there is no shame in that. But you should never profess ignorance when asked to handle the daily fundamentals.

MAXIM 18

HIDE YOUR LOVE OF ACTION MOVIES.

ACTION MOVIES have a proud pedigree. The earliest silent films, such as Buster Keaton's *The General*, featured elaborate and dangerous stunt sequences. The James Bond series, the first *Die Hard* film, Arnold Schwarzenegger dispatching dozens of bad people with a thickly accented quip—pop culture milestones, each and every one.

Those movies' emphasis on explosions and ludicrous plot twists opens them to ridicule by those who profess to love only those motion pictures with niceties such as subtext, realistic characters, and emotional arcs. This is unfair, akin to dismissing all crime novels as pulp and all rock music as unsophisticated. At their best, action films serve as fine examples of how editing, sound, and other fundamentals can play an audience like a well-tuned violin; which is, at its heart, the very reason why filmmakers began committing images to celluloid in the first place.

You can argue that *The Hurt Locker*, the Kathryn Bigelow—directed tale of bomb-disposal experts in Iraq, is most fundamentally an action movie, and it won an Oscar for Best Picture. So did Scorsese's *The Departed*, whose chase scenes and high body count don't exactly qualify it as a genteel drama.

But you can't blame some intellectuals and self-professed film snobs for having a blanket distaste of action movies, any more than you can damn a foodie for refusing to eat anything that comes from a fast-food joint. Everyone has standards, and hundreds of action movies' shoddy scripts and miserable acting make them virtually unwatchable, even as comedy. So if you want your intellectual credentials to remain unassailable, keep your affection for *Dirty Harry* a secret.

THEORY INTO PRACTICE

Being an intellectual and loving action movies aren't mutually exclusive. In fact, you could argue that a love of certain shoot-'em-ups is essential to enjoying both pop and high culture.

However, action movies' reputation as mindless and uncultivated means that, for better or worse, it's probably not in your best interest to shout, "Did you see the way Jason Statham sprayed that terrorist with liquid nitrogen and then punched him in the face, breaking him into a thousand pieces?" at your next intellectual gathering. Nor will listeners necessarily buy your argument that *RoboCop*, underneath its heartwarming tale of a cyborg who perforates a sizable percentage of Detroit's punks with hollow-point bullets, is actually an acerbic comment on urban decay in the Reagan era. Keep the love low-key.

THE INEVITABLE FOOTNOTE

With the passage of time, many movies age into classics and become acceptable to mention in virtually any context. At the time of its 1967 release, *The Dirty Dozen*, which stars Lee Marvin and Charles Bronson on a World War II mission to incinerate a château of Nazi generals, received any number of negative reviews condemning it as visual candy for Neanderthals. More than forty years later, it plays on PBS. The older the movie, the more likely you can enthuse about its action scenes without anyone raising an eyebrow.

MAXIM 19

PASSIONATELY HATE ONE CLASSIC AUTHOR.

PREFERENCES, no matter how outlandish, suggest a sense of taste—and if intellectuals have nothing else, they have taste. After years of devoted scholarship to the art and science of beer drinking, for instance, you may arrive at a place where you love dark stouts, feel totally apathetic toward the paler stuff, and reject any beer that's been spiced. Behind every strong viewpoint, at least in theory, sits a considerable body of experience.

The literary community is no different. Merely uttering the words "Sylvia Plath" at a university get-together will kick off a heated discussion that, depending on the amount of spiced beer consumed, escalates in short order into stunning acts of scholarly rage—someone might even *bang their glass on a table.*

Not that you need to unleash your inner Conan the Barbarian to make a point about literature. But given how intellectuals inevitably harbor well-tended lists of likes and dislikes, *not* confessing a deep hatred of, say, John Milton's poetry will compel other learned types to view you with suspicion.

THEORY INTO PRACTICE

As previously suggested, the surest way to be revealed as a pseudo-intellectual blowhard is to bullshit a viewpoint far beyond your knowledge. And there is no greater bullshit minefield than literature. Position yourself as a literary lion, and sooner or later you will find yourself across the table from someone who wants to talk favorite chapters in *Ulysses.*

Before you can hold an opinion on any one author, you need to read as much of their work as possible: the early stuff, the mid-career stuff, the experimental stuff with letters randomly arranged on the page. You can supplement that with critical essays about the author's style, and pore over guides for those parts you don't quite understand—so long as you read the books themselves.

After a few hundred pages, you're either enjoying the prose, or the very sight of the author's name on a book cover is enough to make you quake in revulsion (there is a middle ground of total indifference, which no wordsmith should aspire to inspire). Congratulations, you now have an informed opinion: nurture and defend it, in the face of those who will inevitably detail the ways in which you're wrong.

Keep in mind that certain writers and books are in vogue irrespective of their actual merit, and that, worse comes to absolute worst, you can always slam your glass down on the bar and tell anyone within earshot that, popular opinion be damned, you think Ken Kesey's *Sometimes a Great Notion* is a far finer piece of literature than his *One Flew Over the Cuckoo's Nest*.

THE INEVITABLE FOOTNOTE

Every author has defenders, some fewer than others. Mention the name "Marquis de Sade" in mixed company, and half the room will cringe with revulsion: the French aristocrat was—how to put this delicately— a bit explicit in his descriptions of perversion, a big part of why his writings continue to attract attention after more than 225 years.

When confronted with an author whom everybody hates, the more altruistic intellectual is sometimes tempted to rally a defense of the poor bugger, whether or not he or she enjoys the actual writing. This is a noble impulse, and helps level out the wild swings of hatred and love that many authors' works endure throughout their public lives. (Granted, it's more difficult to defend Sade, who went out of his way to offend sensibilities.)

FOLLOW MUSEUMS LIKE OTHERS
FOLLOW SPORTS TEAMS.

FROM A TYPICAL WATER-COOLER CONVERSATION about baseball: "Did you see how badly A.J. Burnett sucked last night? He held it together for, what, all of three innings before he fell apart? He really needs to break this slump, it's killing the Yankees."

From a typical conversation at a bar frequented by intellectual types: "Did you see the new Dali show at the Met? I know it's supposed to be the biggest retrospective in years, but they could have been more selective about the pieces they chose. Having that many paintings up is total overload. It wrecks the show."

Like sports teams, many of the major museums live and die by their seasonal lineup. A series of good shows attracts paying visitors, and generates the buzz that draws headlines, sponsorships, and donors. That makes museums, along with films and books and current events, another cultural talking point for the well-rounded intellectual.

THEORY INTO PRACTICE

Museums and galleries aren't exactly secret societies. Newspapers, from the stolid daily to your funky alternative weekly, print reviews of the latest shows. Local news websites will interrupt their white-hot, breaking coverage of a tree limb down on a side road to offer rundowns of upcoming museum events, including film series of talks. You can also direct your browser toward the museum's website, where some intern hopefully stopped "poking" their friends on Facebook—whatever that means—long enough to update the official calendar.

Make a point to see the highest-profile shows, which tend to crop up in conversation with your fellow intellectuals. Take along a small notebook on your jaunts to the local art depositories and fill its pages with details about the works on display: notable artist names, what you find most interesting about certain pieces, and the like.

Those notes aren't meant as grist for future talking points (most of your friends, bless them, couldn't care less about Edo-era samurai armor or a Chuck Close retrospective). The notes help you better absorb the show—once you manage to extract yourself from the crowds. In major cities, the biggest museum shows are flooded in short order by jabbering tourists, creating a human wave that carries you too quickly from gallery to gallery, forcing you to concentrate less on the art and more on throwing well-placed elbows into nearby rib cages.

Aside from the occasional bruise, following along with museums and galleries can be fun. Even if painting and sculpture have never topped your list of interests, even if that piece of "performance art" involving two naked models and a cup makes you wish for a method to erase memories on command, every minute spent on the art scene is further evidence that you are not a Philistine. Becoming a member of a museum or gallery will cement your intellectual *bona fides* still further, and sometimes give you access to shows before they officially open, sparing your elbows and some unfortunate soul's ribs from bruising.

THE INEVITABLE FOOTNOTE

Some museums rotate their shows and events more often than a fashion model changes outfits. Others are far more static. That quaint little gallery with artifacts and etchings from the local Revolutionary War skirmish almost certainly hasn't altered its displays since Gerald Ford kept tripping over the Oval Office trash can.

The same goes for sculpture gardens or transportation museums, since the main attractions tend to weigh a few tons and are thus very immobile. In those cases, you can safely check in every other year or so to see if anything's changed.

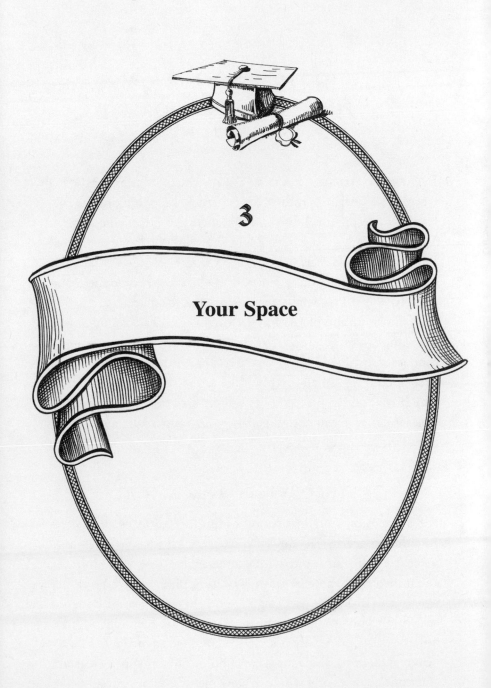

3

Your Space

MAXIM 21

CHOOSE A PROPER LAIR
FOR CONTEMPLATION.

EVERY INTELLECTUAL NEEDS A LAIR in which to brood and contemplate. Hardier types do some of their best thinking in coffee shops, despite the noise and jittery hordes of caffeine addicts. More than a few great works have been written in bars. The Nobel Prize–winning physicist Richard Feynman chose a strip club as a de facto office for jotting notes and equations, something that must have made his wife feel all warm and fuzzy inside.

If those public places have a downside, it's that managers and employees generally frown on you turning a corner of their establishment into your personal hideaway, unless you keep spending a small fortune on espresso or beer—neither of which is good for productivity, albeit for completely opposite reasons. That means establishing your own space away from the world.

THEORY INTO PRACTICE

For academics, your institution's administration usually offers an office space in exchange for your servitude. Whether this space is a large, airy suite with a spectacular view of campus, or a cramped cubbyhole beneath a heating pipe with some rather worrisome BIOHAZARD signage on the wall nearby, depends largely on your position within the campus hierarchy. Win a notable prize, preferably one that comes with a medal or trophy heavy enough to dislocate your shoulder when you pick it up, and your chances of a window view increase exponentially.

If you're not an academic, or if you're a scholar whose department chair has relegated you to a battered metal desk in the library stacks, your best option could involve carving out a space at home. Your lair's most important feature is a door you can close on the world. If your property includes an outbuilding such as an unused shed, a little bit of repair work and judicious pest elimination can turn that into a fantastic workspace. Ideally, there should be ample room to store books, papers, and the like. A place without windows offers a minimum of distractions from mental toil, at the tiny risk of driving you stark raving mad from claustrophobia.

Those living in more cramped conditions—i.e., small apartments in large cities—may need to find office space away from home. You can sometimes rent this cheap, although that could force you to listen as the sweaty salesman in the next space practices his best "It takes *brass balls* to sell real estate" speech to some poor sap on the other end of the phone. Libraries offer quieter space, and access to books, but also a not-so-silent battle for empty chairs and desk space during the busy periods.

If you want to truly customize your intellectual digs, home is likely your best option. It's also the only place where you can nail an inspiring picture to a wall (Einstein sticking his tongue out at the camera, because why not) and not have everyone around you screaming about property damage.

THE INEVITABLE FOOTNOTE

Having a defined space for writing and contemplation isn't a make-or-break requirement for intellectual endeavors. Theorizing and writing can be done in laundry rooms, on park benches, in the front seats of cars during lunch breaks, and pretty much anywhere else you can dodge interacting with others—provided, of course, you're carrying along the necessary tools for preserving your ideas as they come (see Maxim 38: "Keep a paper notebook").

HIGHLIGHT CERTAIN BOOKS
ON YOUR SHELVES.

MILLIONS OF PEOPLE around the world happily obey the whims of what we'll glibly term the design-industrial complex. Did that glossy magazine tell you that mauve is this year's color for your living room? Then mauve it shall be, paired with white trim. And by the way, please do your best to ensure the tableware complements the glassware—those plates with the blue-and-gold rim pair well with your best crystal. Yes. Wonderful. Martha Stewart would positively vibrate with glee at the sight.

Despite this focus on baseboards and paint swatches and bedspreads, few (if any) people devote the same sort of attention to the arrangement of their bookshelves. For the intellectually inclined, this constitutes a serious oversight. Upon entering your home, most other intellectuals will ignore the fine furnishings and make a beeline for your books. If that's not enough to drive you into a quiet frenzy of shelf arrangement, think about how a collection of interesting volumes within arm's reach will save your sanity during a dull conversation with the bland houseguests your significant other invited over for drinks. "Have you read this?" you'll say, lunging toward a particular title like a shipwrecked sailor flailing for a life preserver. "It's a fantastic book. Let me tell you about it. . . ."

In that spirit, it behooves you to think about what the books (and other objects) on your shelves say about you as a thinker.

THEORY INTO PRACTICE

First, you should set your most prized volumes in the general proximity of eye level. Those signed first editions of Cormac McCarthy's *The Border Trilogy*? Place those bad boys right up there. The multivolume set of Giacomo Casanova's *History of My Life*? That likewise deserves some prime real estate, if only to see if any prudes overreact at the sight of the libidinous raconteur's autobiography in such a prominent place.

And then there are . . . the other books. The ones you might enjoy, but which could nonetheless mar your reputation as an intellectual, aspiring or otherwise. If you haven't burned that Dan Brown novel out of shame, it perhaps belongs on your lowermost shelf, behind the potted azalea.

Nor is that the alpha and omega of shelf arrangement. Recall the studies and living rooms of those mega-thinkers in your life: most likely filled not only with books, but also with a few choice artifacts—the tasteful Buddha from that educational expedition to Thailand, for instance, or some sepia-toned photograph snapped a century ago. A sense of timelessness imbues the intellectual's library, untouched by the collective's seasonal interest in mauve or Santa Fe style.

THE INEVITABLE FOOTNOTE

At a certain point, well-endowed shelves reach critical mass, no longer able to contain a rising tide of books. Volumes begin filling cardboard boxes tossed in corners, propping up short table legs, doubling as kindling on winter's most desperate nights. Attempting to impose rhyme or reason on an overflowing collection is pretty much a lost cause, unless a fortuitous house fire allows you to start the collection fresh.

MAXIM 23

PROUDLY DISPLAY
THESE GRAPHIC NOVELS.

COMIC BOOKS are no longer populated only by spandex-clad pituitary accidents slamming each other through walls. No, they have matured. Now they emphasize those small details such as nuanced characterization and emotional motivation that every good writer learns in workshop. Comic books these days are dominated by pituitary accidents intent on *sharing their inner traumas* before they slam each other through walls. As such, they are no longer called *comic books*, but rather the haughtier *graphic novels*.

Thanks to their spandex costuming and legions of younger fans, superheroes prevented the comic book, a rather versatile form when it comes to narrative, from achieving mainstream respect at first.

Over the last two decades, in large part thanks to the efforts of creators like Neil Gaiman and Art Spiegelman, an appreciation for comics as a storytelling medium has grown—and not just because Hollywood's seen fit to adapt pretty much anything ever inked onto a page.

THEORY INTO PRACTICE

The exact definition of a graphic novel is a subject of intense debate among those who study such things. These illustrated narratives tend to be significantly longer than "regular" comic books, which often number around twenty-odd pages, and they feature traditional bookbinding. Sometimes they offer a stand-alone story, created expressly by the artist and writer for a longer format; other graphic novels collect a set of previously published comics into a single narrative arc.

The following graphic novels all helped the medium gain that elusive respect, by offering narratives that qualify as fine literature, combined with artwork that's frame-worthy. And yes, some do feature superheroes in spandex.

Maus: Art Spiegelman's account of his parents' survival in Nazi Europe (split into two volumes, although you can find them collected as one) is one of the most harrowing depictions of the Holocaust committed to paper. The book won the Pulitzer Prize.

American Splendor: Harvey Pekar wrote a series of autobiographical comics about his life as a hospital file clerk in Cleveland. His portraits of the daily grind are about as far from superpowers and masks as you can get: bitter at moments, often funny, and sometimes touching (particularly the *Our Cancer Year* story arc).

Sandman: Neil Gaiman's comic series about the Lord of Dreams (referred to, among other names, as Dream and Morpheus) is a fantastical phantasmagoria, the kind that draws on centuries of literary influences and earns a whole host of awards.

Watchmen: Written by Alan Moore, and illustrated by Dave Gibbons, this graphic novel did its utter best to subvert the superhero genre, making its costumed characters deeply flawed and filling the narrative with an ice-water dose of Cold War paranoia. In the twenty-five years since its publication, endless waves of writers and illustrators have tried to match its nihilism and expert control of subtext, with few (if any) successes.

Sin City: Frank Miller's red-meat ode to classic pulp fiction will offend more delicate sensibilities. Everybody else can stay for the master class in black-and-white illustration, not to mention the rogue's gallery of criminals, psychopaths, fallen angels, and hit-men shouting memorably hard-boiled dialogue.

THE INEVITABLE FOOTNOTE

As previously mentioned, comics featuring costumed heroes have mutated (somewhat) to offer stories of greater moral complexity. Nonetheless, if you place a collected volume of Spider-Man or X-Men comics on a prominent shelf—and especially alongside your titans of literature—chances are pretty good a visiting intellectual will arch an eyebrow and prod you into defending that choice of reading matter. At that point, you can shrug and say, "Well, I like comics." Just don't resort to POW-style fisticuffs to back up your choices.

MAXIM 24

INCLUDE ART FILMS IN YOUR
MOVIE COLLECTION.

INTELLECTUALS-IN-TRAINING often spend an inordinate amount of time refining their book collections, and not nearly enough time refining their film collections. The cumulative effect of ten feet of Russian great authors (Chekhov, Nabokov, Gogol, Pushkin, Dostoyevsky, and—because we want to ensure those shelves creak under the weight of all that paper—Tolstoy) can be undermined, in an instant, by the nearby presence of the *Transformers* trilogy in widescreen high-definition.

If a film includes explosions, Victoria's Secret supermodels in their "acting" debut, Oscar winners slumming as moustache-twirling villains in order to make a mortgage payment on their place in Barbados, car chases, actors so stiff they appear created by computer graphics, and vampires, it will almost certainly entertain the thirteen-year-old in your life. But it probably won't win you points with any intellectuals perusing your disc collection. An "intellectual" film collection includes titles that challenge you to think, where the director was clearly more interested in creating a personal statement rather than the largest gasoline explosion ever committed to celluloid: art films, a term that encompasses both those tiny works that played for two weeks at your local avant-garde theater, and the more popular works whose creators pushed the expectations of the form.

THEORY INTO PRACTICE

When it comes to the exact films that belong on the intellectual movie-shelf (or intellectual movie hard-drive, if you've gone completely digital), no firm guidelines apply. As with books, knowledge of what constitutes good film is something developed over a lifetime of viewing lots of movies, and not only the critically lauded ones. You can learn a lot from watching a truly atrocious B-flick, often because its sheer ineptitude re-educates you in all the little things, like coherent editing and a halfway decent story, that you usually take for granted.

Watching more notable art-house films will provide you with talking points the next time you encounter an aficionado with a burning desire to talk symbolism in the latest Terrence Malick flick. The works of Woody Allen (particularly *Annie Hall*, his best attempt at being Woody Allen), Martin Scorsese (*Raging Bull*, a master class in film and sound editing, all in service of portraying its main character's seriously wounded psyche), Alfred Hitchcock (*Psycho*, the maestro director's most virtuoso performance), Francis Ford Coppola (*The Godfather*, Parts I and II—there is no third), Krzysztof Kieslowski (*The Decalogue*, a ten-part exploration of the Ten Commandments that manages to be wry, bleak, and deep—sometimes all in the same scene), François Truffaut (*The 400 Blows*, whose camerawork inspired a generation of filmmakers), and David Lynch (*Blue Velvet*, the champagne of cinematic weirdness) constitute a good start, and the tip of a very large iceberg.

For those who aren't cinema fans but need a few discs for the lair, consider obtaining films that meet at least two of the following criteria: subtitles, three-hour-plus running times, scenes set in icy foreign countries, impenetrable plots, climaxes that feature characters engaging in heavy philosophical discussion over a bottle of something high-proof, and a soundtrack by Björk. (Bad movies can also offer some or all of these elements; they often double as a convenient cure for insomnia.)

THE INEVITABLE FOOTNOTE

Stock at least one guilty-pleasure movie among your collection. Scientists have wide leverage in this category, which allows them to shelf sci-fi flicks such as *Aliens* and *Terminator* without anyone blinking an eye.

MAXIM 25

ARRANGE YOUR DESK AREA TO
SUGGEST PURE BRILLIANCE.

THE INTELLECTUAL WORKS best in a customized space. Some writers refuse to compose unless their desk contains certain charms arranged just so. Scientists and inventors need their journals and diagrams close at hand. Artists keep the local paper-supply store in business with repeated trips for new notebooks, which they squirrel away in any available cubbyhole.

The intellectual workspace also features epic amounts of clutter, signifying a Mind at Work. Newton generated voluminous amounts of notes, at least until his dog accidentally set much of it on fire. Princeton administrators continue to find fossilized students underneath the mountains of papers left behind by Einstein. Writers, musicians, philosophers, technologists, and innovators of every stripe leave debris in their wake, as they power from idea to idea. You should do no less.

There is an art to arranging the area around your desk in a way that shows both your intellectual aptitude and your ability to wrestle with a multitude of projects at once. In addition to skillfully designed clutter, the strategic placement of some other objects will ensure that anyone entering your space will instantly know they're in the presence of a mental titan.

THEORY INTO PRACTICE

The art of arranging your desk in order to fulfill these goals is a delicate one.

Clutter: Some intellectuals organize their mess—that is, their material—using the *zonal approach*, subdivided by year or subject: journals on this part of the desk, files in this drawer, maybe all papers into those boxes shoved in the kneehole. Others take the *geologic layer approach*: the newest document for editing, or paper for reading, takes a prime spot in the small clearing in the middle of the desk. Once tossed aside, that not-so-new material finds its way onto a pile of slightly older stuff beside the trash can, which sits atop even older stuff in turn. (Maxim 26, "Design a fail-safe organizing system," offers some additional tips for staring your clutter down.)

Books: Nothing suggests an intellectual mind at full throttle like shelves and piles of books. Reference texts (dictionary, thesaurus, and, for added points, a foreign-language dictionary) belong stacked on the desk, alongside one or two generously dog-eared and bookmarked volumes related to your field of study. For the nearby shelves, arrange your books per Maxim 22 ("Highlight certain books on your shelves").

Production Tool: Whether notebook, tablet, or laptop, it should sit at the center of your desk, signifying your readiness to jot down the next great idea. (For artists, this "tool" might be a drawing pad or lump of sculpting material.)

The Talismans: Every intellectual has one. It could be a favorite pen, a tiny Buddha statue bought in a Bangkok marketplace, a framed photo of your kid, or some combination of objects. It personalizes your space, hinting at the human being behind the brain.

THE INEVITABLE FOOTNOTE

Clutter, while impressive, places the information you value at risk. Who knows what vital papers or notebooks could be lost deep in the clutter-mountain, or inadvertently tossed away by the irate spouse? The solution is to keep the *truly* important things in their own separate area or drawer. Financial documents should be placed in their own little Fort Knox, away from the rest of the bric-a-brac.

MAXIM 26

DESIGN A FAIL-SAFE
ORGANIZING SYSTEM.

So you've created a lair and managed to accumulate a metric ton of books and paper. Nobody dares enter your sanctuary, for fear they might accidentally crush a torn-out notebook page with the secrets of the universe written on it. Congratulations. (The smell is a bit disturbing.) Now comes the tricky part: if you want the space and its contents to contribute to your intellectual endeavors, you need an easy way to find information when needed.

As mentioned in Maxim 25 ("Arrange your desk area to suggest pure brilliance"), some intellectuals develop a psychic connection with their clutter. They seem to know the location of every scrap of paper, including that issue of *Granta* from 1992 they plan to reference in their latest essay. In the category of Useless Superpowers, that's a pretty decent one: but it's probably better if you create and refine your own system, the better to find things in a timely (and stress-free) manner.

THEORY INTO PRACTICE

The Great Purge: You are not your stuff. Tyler Durden offered that philosophy in *Fight Club*, and you can adopt it as your mantra as you steel yourself for the most painful experience this side of shaving off every inch of body hair with a dull razor: tossing out papers no longer of use. Yes, it will hurt. Yes, it is necessary. A leaner and meaner space does wonders for your sanity.

Everybody Needs Routine: Establish a routine for anything new entering your space: an in-box to handle papers that need your attention, perhaps a box for unread books, a separate area reserved for keys and other small objects easily lost, and so on. Sticking with these patterns will streamline your daily life.

Shred: Shred your financial documents to prevent identity theft. Unless you want your good name swiped by a three-hundred-pound ex-convict with serious tattoo and daddy issues, who uses it to finance a multistate run from the law—the sort of thing that makes home loans and airport-security checkpoints an awkward experience for the rest of your life—make sure bank statements and anything with your social security number on them end up as itty-bitty bits of paper.

Streamline Those Files: If you keep telling yourself that the BBQ takeout menu with an interesting doodle on the margin, the Henry James quote scrawled on the back of a map of Florence, and all the other scraps and notes could one day come in handy, you're being delusional. This is how people transform into hoarders. Keep a separate, isolated file for random crap, and throw out its contents on a regular basis.

Digitize What You Can: Thanks to the Web, you can upload everything from documents to photos to the digital cloud. This removes a lot of the need for paper. Digitize as much of your media as possible, and have a cleaner space as a result. Added bonus: most online storage allows you to search through years' worth of content.

THE INEVITABLE FOOTNOTE

Some people are so relentlessly efficient that they have no need for an organization system. Their desk consists of an unmarked calendar, an empty inbox, and a shelf of generic family photos. Their space is free of mess and dust. These "people" are aliens sent to observe our habits.

MAXIM 27

BUY BOOKS BY THE FOOT.

WE ACCUMULATE BOOKS over a lifetime. Some favorite titles we read once a year, or certain passages once a day. Other books we neglect on the shelf, unread for years, reduced to mere decoration, gathering dust, their authors' sweat and blood and toil left unacknowledged and wasted—

Ahem, yes. Anyway. The one thing that unifies intellectuals across time and cultures, aside from the thirst for knowledge and the occasional eccentricity, is the library in their abodes and offices. The next time your local church or school hosts a book sale, swing by and watch for any customers shuffling for the register with a tower of hardcover volumes in their trembling arms. Those people have stumbled onto the secret for rapidly building a collection for the ages: buying in bulk, cheaply. If you're an intellectual, you need a substantial book collection, preferably at a cost that will leave you with a few extra dollars for food. Here's how to build one:

THEORY INTO PRACTICE

In addition to school and church sales, where you can sometimes purchase books for pennies on the dollar, the other best venue is used bookstores, which sell their wares at a significant discount. Scour these hunting grounds early and often: the intellectual on the prowl for texts is a coyote or hyena, a scavenger genetically incapable of giving up.

There's just one little drawback: despite its best efforts, some nights the scavenging animal can find little better than a small bone with some dry gristle on it. Used bookstores and garage sales offer books by the ton, true, but most of them are titles nobody wants to read anymore: yesteryear's bestsellers, nonfiction books rendered hopelessly out-of-date by subsequent editions, how-to books that obviously didn't how-to enough. These scuffed, dog-eared orphans await your judgment. Do you really need a Tom Clancy novel from 1988, or a third copy of Merriam-Webster's Pocket Dictionary?

Unless you own a bar with wall-to-wall bookshelves that need filling, the answer is "No." A more efficient solution, as with so many things, is often found online: websites like Amazon.com and Alibris.com that deal in printed knowledge for as low as 99 cents per volume. If you're willing to pay the shipping, you can find and order a specific book within three or four mouse-clicks. Such are the glories of the Internet, where everything you desire is always for sale: the hardcover of Cormac McCarthy's *All the Pretty Horses*, a lightly soiled futon, or a dude who'll do anything for ten bucks.

THE INEVITABLE FOOTNOTE

There are books worth buying in their pristine, original condition. A first edition of something great, signed by the author? As an investment, it might not be worth the equivalent of a Porsche in twenty years (in fact, making rare books a significant part of your retirement plan is a mistake on par with depositing your cash with Bernie Madoff), but think of the bragging rights when you show off that inside flap on which Norman Mailer, with infinite care and precision, wrote your name followed by "Up yours, punk."

MAXIM 28

CURATE YOUR LIQUOR CABINET.

LIKE THE BOOKSHELF, the liquor cabinet or sideboard is another opportunity for the intellectual to display his informed choices on a particular subject.

Why liquor? First and foremost, guests tend to gravitate toward it. Individual tastes diverge from there: some are perfectly happy with a six-pack of light beer, while others turn their noses up at nothing less than Johnnie Walker Blue Label (the champagne of whiskies) or Champagne (the Champagne of, er, yeah).

Second, like literature and other intellectual pursuits, liquor has long proved a mainstay of civilization. According to a theory expounded by a close friend over a couple bottles of Iron City Beer (arguably Pittsburgh's finest export), the ancients first got together on the plains in order to brew and drink alcohol. Soon, so many people had gathered that the collective had no choice but to build shelters, thus birthing the first cities. Everything great that's happened since—writing, architecture, mathematics, the internal combustion engine, Angelina Jolie—is the direct result of a group of our hairy ancestors, after a hard week of spearing deer and fighting tooth and nail for access to the nearest pond, wanting to get their buzz on.

When it comes to actually stocking said liquor cabinet, there exist precious few hard rules. A significant number of history's most famous intellects enjoyed nothing more than explaining their latest theories over a glass of pretty much anything even remotely alcoholic, and damn the taste. Nonetheless, the intellectual who enjoys knowledge for knowledge's sake, in all possible categories, might do well to cultivate an interest in liquors that expand your palate, as opposed to merely wrecking your brain cells.

On that note, please remember to drink responsibly. You don't want to wake up in the morning stinking like Plato, that sop.

THEORY INTO PRACTICE

As mentioned, part of satisfying a curiosity about alcohol involves stocking a diverse liquor cabinet, especially if you play host on a regular basis. Some staples to consider:

Vodka: A Russian diminutive for "little water," vodka is a distilled spirit whose essentially tasteless nature renders it the multitool of mixed drinks: from screwdrivers (a dash of vodka mixed with a whole lot of orange juice; or, for your friends, a whole lot of vodka with a dash of orange juice) to a White Russian (vodka combined with coffee liquor and cream), there's precious little vodka can't do to help you get through the endless winter night of the soul.

Absinthe: The French bohemians of the late-nineteenth and early-twentieth centuries, including the painter Henri de Toulouse-Lautrec, swore by this spirit derived from wormwood and other ingredients. Lauded for its supposedly psychotropic effects, absinthe was also damned and banned in much of Europe and the United States for that reason. In the past several years it's undergone something of a revival, allowing modern audiences to discover that, despite the legends, nothing in that green liquid will make you see fairies. It's sometimes useful to keep a bottle around as a talking point, particularly for fans of *fin de siècle* Paris.

Whiskey: The favored beverage of Southern poets and those pretending to be Southern poets, this aged hard liquor from grain mash has a centuries-long history and a proud reputation (disparage scotch in the wrong Scottish bar, and prepare to run for your life).

Ether: Part of Hunter S. Thompson's substance collection on his infamous trip to Las Vegas. Not recommended for any life forms not Hunter S. Thompson.

Beer: Recent years have seen an increased focus on the microbrews produced by smaller breweries. Many are excellent. Others are largely indistinguishable from mass-produced commercial brews. A sad few taste like Charles Bukowski's piss. Lovers of the esoteric will appreciate having a microbrew on hand in place of a regular beer, but take care not to bullshit any beer snobs who will want to talk about "bock" and "bottom fermenting."

THE INEVITABLE FOOTNOTE

A refrigerator stocked with several types of "light beer" does not qualify as a "diverse liquor cabinet."

MAXIM 29

KEEP YOUR WALLS FREE OF DEGREES AND HUNTING TROPHIES.

A BARE WALL just begs for something to be hung upon it, and if you have any ego at all, you'll be tempted to hang something that reflects one of your accomplishments. Hunters with a sense of tradition will display the stuffed heads of beasts they've killed. Scholars often nail up their master's or doctorate degrees, as a trophy of twenty years' worth of schooling and another thirty years of paying off loans. Medals and awards assume places of honor in a home or office, although your competitive-eating trophy will draw a few odd stares for its ridiculously lifelike rendering of a man with fifteen hotdogs in his mouth.

There is nothing unnatural about wanting to display your life's high points on the walls. The Egyptian pharaohs had their accomplishments chiseled on the stone panels of tombs. What possible drawback to displaying a photo of you shaking hands with a prominent federal judge, especially if your bond of friendship was forever cemented that night you helped him hide that hooker's body?

Absolutely nothing: except that, after a certain point (say, three photographs of you with famous people, or a hanging bear pelt large enough to cover a family of five) those wall furnishings detract from the intellectual's carefully crafted image of someone more concerned with the life of the mind than life's baubles and honors, unless the baubles in question are the National Book Award and the Presidential Medal of Freedom.

THEORY INTO PRACTICE

As with so many things in the intellectual life, minimalism is key. Acknowledge life's rewards with a handful of tastefully chosen objects, but decline to place them front and center for general admiration. If you want to decorate a room in a way that suggests you're a quality *Homo sapiens*, at least in the mental department, stack it with shelves of books. If you've written books yourself, make sure to place them at eye level: that will ultimately draw more admiration (and envy) than a photo of you with Bill Clinton, because that dude reportedly got around.

THE INEVITABLE FOOTNOTE

Lawyers and doctors use their office walls to hang degrees from impressive institutions. Particularly in the latter's case, this is a positive thing: if a surgeon plans on cutting you open for a tricky five-hour operation involving many delicate organs and tissue-paper-thin blood vessels, you'd prefer to see he learned his trade at a reputable institution such as Harvard Medical School, as opposed to Big Bob's House of Slicin' Good.

MAXIM 30

DISDAIN DESIGN FADS.

NEVER UNDERESTIMATE HUMANKIND'S OBSESSION with novelty. The urge to see, hold, and purchase the newest thing has fueled the career of everyone from P.T. Barnum to Steve Jobs.

Whether iPhones or fake mermaids, novelty powers designers to offer up new lines every season. A barrage of marketing ramps up the pressure to buy, buy, buy—and then the next year, to buy, buy, and buy again.

This is a trap. Design fads inevitably transition to newer fads, because designers have their own impeccably tailored spawn to feed. For the intellectual, the temptation to purchase the latest electronics, fashion trifles, or other accessories is often a strong one; as if owning those items could help emphasize your uniqueness, and thus your intelligence and sense of taste, from the rest of the herd. But pursuing the latest styles wastes money better devoted to books, and mental energy better put to other uses.

THEORY INTO PRACTICE

The poorly dressed professor is a perpetual cliché, yet holds an element of truth. Out there in the world right now, a lecturer is wearing a yellow-and-blue checked sport coat with worn elbows. Does he know the garment violates every precept of good taste and stylish design? Absolutely, and nor does he care. On campus, that sort of clothing decision is a badge of perverse pride, a sign that you're focused on bigger things.

A similar rule governs your personal space. The aesthetic quality of the intellectual's lair is beholden to the books and artifacts that line the walls, the papers that accrue, the interesting tidbits above the door frame, and a hodgepodge of furniture. The space serves as a stage for the owner's current interests and obsessions, as opposed to any chichi *du jour*.

You're an intellectual: you don't have the time or interest in making sure your socks match. Go forth and wear that mismatched pair with pride.

THE INEVITABLE FOOTNOTE

The design student, aspiring to walk in the footsteps of the greats, might study his or her contemporaries' work by purchasing and then dissecting it. Under those circumstances, it's perfectly acceptable to embrace design trends, if only in the name of creating something exciting and new.

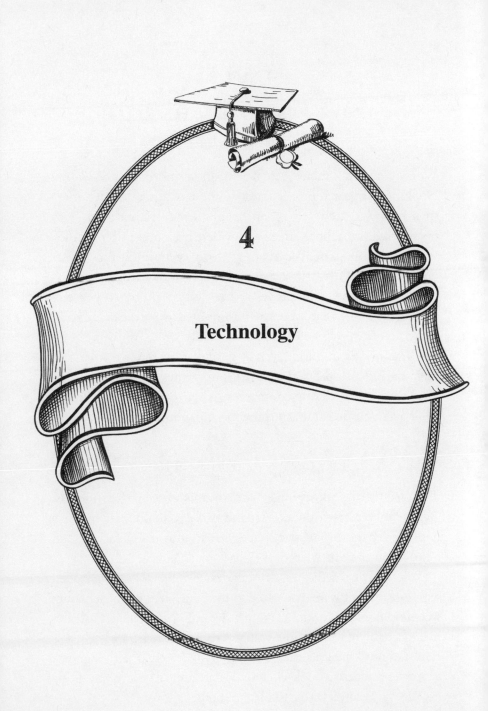

4

Technology

MAXIM 31

CARRY E-BOOKS ON THE ROAD.

WHEN E-READERS such as Amazon's Kindle and Barnes & Noble's Nook first appeared on the market, and customers seemed more than happy to read text on an "e-ink" screen rather than crack open a traditional book, trees everywhere breathed a sigh of relief.

So did your spine. Per Maxim 1, "Carry an intellectual book (at all times)," the world-class thinker is never without a tome in hand. That tome often proves rather hefty. And when you end up hefting more than one, their combined weight can threaten to twist your vertebrae worse than a bendy straw. While upholding Maxim 1 is important for any intellectual (not to mention their dating prospects), an exception comes into play during long trips and arduous commutes, when carrying an e-reader will spare you the strain of those extra paper-pounds.

THEORY INTO PRACTICE

The weight of your average hardcover is around 1.7 pounds, give or take a few ounces. A paperback? Usually just under a pound, depending on size, paper stock, and other factors. An e-book, on the other hand, weighs zero.

Whether on a dedicated e-reader device, tablet, or laptop loaded with e-reader software, you can cart the equivalent of an elephant's weight in books without breaking a sweat. For the intellectual who makes a habit of toting more volumes than a library on wheels, this can be, if not a lifesaver, then certainly a life *improver* (although not a muscle-builder: e-book aficionados are denied the upper-body exercise that comes with a full bag of books).

THE INEVITABLE FOOTNOTE

The book in its basic form—sheets of pulped trees printed with ink and sandwiched between two covers—has survived the ravages of time, evolving technology, the occasional mass burning, and the *Twilight* series. A book is cheap to make and own, capable of surviving a long drop, useful as an impromptu tool, and replaceable if you lose it. It looks handsome, smells good, needs no batteries, and fills out a shelf nicely.

A book, once reduced to a handful of bits stored on a hard drive, loses all these fine qualities. An e-reader is also vulnerable to falls, spilled water glasses, and a lack of battery power.

The more technologically inclined will argue that the ability to access infinite texts with a button-click far outweighs these drawbacks. To that, a bibliophile will likely retort with a sigh of resignation, hoist that book bag with its five pounds of hardcover volumes onto a creaking shoulder, and shuffle off to work or class. E-books are indeed convenient, and may save you a small fortune in chiropractor bills, but others will argue that a traditional book is worth the weight.

MAXIM 32

EDIT YOUR FACEBOOK PROFILE
TO TELL THE RIGHT STORY.

AH, SOCIAL-NETWORKING SITES. However did we stalk our exes, er, keep in touch with friends before them? Hundreds of millions of people have profiles on social networks like Facebook, updating them daily with images and witty missives, and yet a significant percentage of such people remain ambivalent about the prospect of maintaining a public presence online. "I hate this thing; I'm going to quit," they might say. "By the way, did you see the pix from the party this weekend? Isn't what Bob did to that gerbil illegal?"

No matter how much you grouse, it's highly unlikely that social networks will fade away anytime soon. This can work to the intellectual's advantage, provided you tailor your online identity. Think of your social-networking profile as a way to extend an image of yourself to the world, complete with an instant summary of your favorite books (weighty), films (subtitled), and activities (put down "nightlong discussions of modern existentialism" as a mating call to other intellectuals).

THEORY INTO PRACTICE

Creating an intellectual social-networking profile is largely a matter of editing your online photos with extreme prejudice. Those candid shots of you unconscious in a bathtub filled with liquor bottles? Delete. The concert shot from your hairstyle-inappropriate years in the Guns N' Roses cover band? Delete.

Any images of you in clown makeup, or shaking hands with Charlie Sheen, or dressed in a leotard, or anything taken in Cabo: banish them to the digital void, forever.

At the same time, emphasize the intellectual elements. A photo of you standing beside a particularly notable scholar is a prime candidate for your profile image, along with any shot taken in the context of books, art, or a building with Grecian columns. Actual details are of secondary importance, as your ultimate goal here is quick impressions of scholarliness. Nobody looks at their friends' online photos for more than a few seconds anyway, unless they're stunned by what happened to the gerbil.

THE INEVITABLE FOOTNOTE

When constructing your social-networking profile, consider how less information (and fewer photos) linked to your name means less data for marketers and other companies to use for their own nefarious ends, not to mention fewer potential errors for your friends (or "Friends") to call you on. Come to think of it, your best option for a suitable profile may involve posting a photo of Sigmund Freud as your "portrait," leaving everything else blank, and swearing henceforth to conduct any correspondence via pen and paper.

CAST LOL AND EMOTICONS FROM YOUR LEXICON.

THERE IS A VERY SPECIAL PLACE in Hell reserved for whoever created the emoticon. Nor can we blame the scourge solely on text messaging and e-mail: as far back as the nineteenth century, writers ended their sentences with a colon and parentheses perverted into a frowny or smiley face. No less an eminent figure than Abraham Lincoln may have deployed a ;) in an 1862 speech, something that scholars have stridently insisted was a typo and not a sign that one of our nation's most revered presidents surrendered to the temptation to punctuate like a fourteen-year-old girl.

Then again, Lincoln won the Civil War, so he can perhaps be forgiven if that emoticon was an intentional one. But if you didn't save a nation from tearing itself apart, and if you're not a teenager with a phone and a pair of hyperactive thumbs, then eliminating emoticons from your writing lexicon is probably in everyone's best interest.

The maxim also applies to abbreviations such as LOL, LMAO, OMG, BRB, and their ilk. Centuries from now, future historians will pore over any e-mail printouts we've left behind, and marvel at the strange codes we used to communicate with one another. They'll wonder: What do these arcane letters mean? What incredible subtext and nuance do they convey? Little will they know that LOL was meant only to convey the knee-slapping, gut-busting hilarity of yet another photo of a kitten dressed in a top hat. Even if it means spending a few additional minutes composing a phrase or paragraph, an intellectual prefers to deploy actual words in the name of nuanced arguments and insights, instead of relying on the blunt instrument of OMG LMAO BFN.

THEORY INTO PRACTICE

Emoticons likely originated out of distrust and fear in the power of the written word. The hesitant writer, unsure if "I had a great weekend" truly conveys that they had a *great* weekend, is inclined to tap out a :-) after the period.

Have faith in words to convey your point. If you feel a sentence is somehow ambiguous, rewrite it for greater clarity. After that, if your hesitation persists, feel free to add another sentence (or two) to buttress the first one: "I had a great weekend. Really. I'm serious." That could add a whole three seconds to the time it takes to type your message, a collective sacrifice we'll have to make as a nation in order to eliminate the horror of emoticons once and for all.

THE INEVITABLE FOOTNOTE

In 1969, an interviewer reportedly asked Vladimir Nabokov to place himself among the ranks of writers, living and dead. "I often think there should exist a special typographical sign for a smile," he replied. "Some sort of concave mark, a supine round bracket, which I would now like to trace in reply to your question."

One could argue that, if Nabokov condoned the use of an emoticon as a way to sidestep graceless questions, then such typography should be available for anyone's use. That being said, it's also highly probable that the author of *Lolita* was being a little bit sardonic in that instance. ;-)

MAXIM 34

TWITTER YOUR BRILLIANCE.

SHORT MESSAGES are arguably a more popular form than ever. People tap out texts on their phones, and compose 140-character tweets on Twitter. If a haiku master found himself magically transported from seventeenth-century Japan to the current day, his first question would probably be, "What is this drivel?"

Unlike the haiku master, who agonizes over every syllable and word, the substantial majority of these Twitter dispatches aren't the result of careful deliberation:

"Hw UR u? Hahaha. J/K."

Confronted with that massacre of language, our transported poet might simply draw his sword, the better to skewer the offending device. (Intellectuals of past eras were often willing to settle philosophical points with weaponry as well as with words.) Yet swordplay would fail to halt the universal tendency to hack and chop words into tiny bits, all in the name of speed and convenience.

Which leaves it up to you, the intellectual, to push back against this messy texting trend in the only way that doesn't leave you open to charges of property destruction: by ensuring your own texts and tweets are well thought out and worthy of reading.

THEORY INTO PRACTICE

As with any lingo, text abbreviations (BTW, B4) are largely impenetrable to outsiders, and there is little point in staying fluent in what the great intellectual Hank Moody once called "a proto-language that resembles more what cavemen used to speak than the King's English." When writing your brief messages (whether texting or tweeting), type out whole words, and pay attention to those niggling little details like punctuation, grammar, and spelling. If this proves frustrating, tell yourself that your life's highest calling is to defend the sanctity of language—and to convey useful information.

In doing so, you'll stand out from the pack who rely on this incredible technology to tell the world about the fish taco they ate for lunch.

For the intellectual, Twitter represents an opportunity to expose a larger audience to your emerging brilliance. Discovered an interesting quote? Tweet it out. Published an article or blog posting in need of reading? Tweet that, too. Want to comment on some vital issue? You can send several tweets for that one. Ensure each 140-character missive either informs or improves lives. Nobody cares about that taco's failure to play nice with your stomach.

THE INEVITABLE FOOTNOTE

Intellectuals may find communication with their children impossible except via text. Driven to extremes, desperate to connect in a way their progeny will understand, and willing to hate themselves afterward, the mental titan may resort to the occasional 'W2M' or 'WAN2TLK.'

MAXIM 35

DECIDE ON THE PROPER QUOTE FOR YOUR E-MAIL SIGNATURE.

IN LIEU OF THE HANDWRITTEN LETTER, now mostly reserved for special occasions like begging your loved one to come back and bring the dog, please baby I'm sorry, the bulk of everyday communication is by e-mail.

E-mail is both a gift and a curse. E-mail is instant. You don't send it from New York on Monday and get it in San Francisco on Friday. It's cheap. You don't need to buy stamps. And you can delete it with the click of a button, sparing you from walking all the way to the trash can. At the same time, e-mail lacks personality. Unlike handwriting, the default typeface and font are utterly boring. Attempts to decorate it bring to mind truisms like "lipstick on a pig."

You can transcend this sterility by placing a borrowed quote below your signature and contact information. "The only thing necessary for the triumph of evil is for good men to do nothing," a quote attributed to the Irish statesman Edmund Burke, is one often deployed to suggest the e-mail writer's breadth of knowledge and iron moral stance when it comes to communicating with the landlord about rent.

However, overused quotes have an annoying tendency to backfire. They suggest less that the e-mail writer is a scholarly mastermind, and more that such writers spent five minutes online searching for famous quotations to make themselves sound smart. As with so many things, the art is in the little details.

THEORY INTO PRACTICE

Your e-mail signature makes the most sense when it mirrors your profession. A politician with an urge for bipartisanship, for example, might choose this one attributed to Franklin D. Roosevelt: "I'm not the smartest fellow in the world, but I can sure pick smart colleagues."

Or a musician might opt for something along the lines of Gustav Mahler's "If a composer could say what he had to say in words he would not bother trying to say it in music."

Avoid quotes that suggest some inner turmoil on your part, particularly as it pertains to gaining new knowledge. "Deep experience is never peaceful" is a Henry James quote that makes frequent appearances online, but its suggestion of philosophical distress remains inappropriate for an e-mail wondering whether lunch should kick off at noon or twelve-thirty.

Along the same lines: when judging the respective merits of two quotes, opt for the one that seems funny and less profound. Nelson Mandela's "Let there be work, bread, water, and salt for all" is a noble sentiment but, like the James quote, so heavy it will crack the flimsy backbone of everyday correspondence. Instead, something like William Alger's "We give advice by the bucket but take it by the grain" is more likely to draw an appreciative chuckle, and not overshadow your message.

THE INEVITABLE FOOTNOTE

An e-mail signature isn't a necessary part of correspondence, and many choose to leave their messages free of quotes. The intellectual in business life may opt for a signature that includes his or her full formal name, e-mail address, office phone, cell phone, fax, physical address, and website, but neglect the penetrating insight into human morality.

MAXIM 36

SELECT A RINGTONE THAT SUGGESTS ACTUAL TASTE IN MUSIC.

Too often, you find yourself in a meeting or lecture when a cell phone starts blaring a bubbly pop hit. If everybody in the room is an adult, the next few moments prove embarrassing for whomever scrambles to silence the device. No matter how quickly they do so, the damage is done: the institute's senior director of economic theory is revealed now and forever as a closet lover of boy bands or J-pop.

The worse alternative is when the device's owner, stunned by this accidental disclosure of poor musical taste, decides to do nothing and let the tone stop on its own. (No way will they admit to loving the same music as their fourteen-year-old daughter. *No way.*) So everyone sits there, conversation at a standstill, as the collective embarrassment stretches each second, Theory of Relativity–style, into roughly a thousand years.

An intellectual can't insist to have downloaded a poppy ringtone in an ironic frame of mind—phones can be many things, but ironic isn't one of them. Please adjust your sound accordingly, choosing a bit of music that reflects an intellectual's refined and sensible tastes.

THEORY INTO PRACTICE

The intellectual's approach to music, including that ten-second clip that announces an incoming call, is similar to that of books or movies: appreciative of innovation and genius, and not annoying.

In that spirit, music to consider:

Jazz/Blues Greats: A former colleague of mine chose a selection from Miles Davis's "Sketches of Spain" as his smartphone ringtone. It was an inspired choice: elegant, smooth, neatly conveying the jazz musician's genius in but a few seconds. Jazz greats (Charlie Parker, Duke Ellington, et al.) and blues legends (Robert Johnson, for one) deliver tunes with similar qualities.

Classical: The soft hum of violins, the graceful tinkling of a piano, the horns' throaty moan: a symphony, even on a phone with the volume turned high, is never jarring—unless you select the opening of the first movement of Beethoven's Fifth Symphony. For best results, think something quieter along the lines of Vivaldi.

Brian Eno: The rocker's ambient *Music for Airports* is distinctive but, with its drifting piano and electronic loops, quite restrained. If it can soothe a terminal full of anxious travelers, it likely won't offend anyone within earshot.

THE INEVITABLE FOOTNOTE

You love annoying pop, and absolutely refuse to consider another option for your ringtone—it wouldn't be authentic. Go ahead, make everyone's day: load it up. Just be prepared to face the consequences.

MAXIM 37

BEWARE OF SPELL CHECK.

SPELL CHECK IS THE DEVIL'S WORK. Like many things that sow hatred and destruction in their wake, spell check was created with the finest intentions: some well-meaning software engineer wanted to alert writers to spelling errors in a document. Once spell check became an integral part of word-processing programs, people began speeding through their compositions without a second glance, trusting it to catch any errors. It didn't. Whether "illicit" in place of "elicit," or "two" instead of "too," the software failed to nab correctly spelled words used in error, much less any grammatical car wrecks.

In order to deal with the latter problem, those kind engineers gave spell check a large and slightly slow-witted brother: grammar check. It proved equally fallible. Not only does grammar check fail to catch some ingrown sentences and phrases, it sometimes snatches the technically correct ones and refuses to let go, no matter how many times you click "Ignore." Now the two prowl the wilds of your document like a pair of evil moonshiners straight out of *Deliverance*, hollering at anything that looks funny and generally causing you at least one annoyance every fifteen minutes.

The intellectual distrusts the two brothers, and makes a point to reread important documents for errors, regardless of what spell check or grammar check think. The truly intellectual might turn off these features entirely, trusting that they know when to reach for the Webster's or Strunk & White. Spell check won't catch when you accidentally type "We can do that shorty" instead of "We can do that shortly," and thus won't save you when that e-mail's height-challenged and temperamental recipient starts plotting revenge.

THEORY INTO PRACTICE

Here are a few traditional trouble spots for spell check and its idiot sibling:

Name Spellings: If documents are the grammatical equivalent of those spooky temples from the Indiana Jones movies, then proper name spellings are the treasure rooms where the fake floors collapse, tumbling you into a pit filled with unhygienic spikes and some very irate scorpions. Spell check is generally terrible with names that are either (a) not famous or (b) longer than one syllable. When confronted with a document filled with long and complicated names, such as the Moscow phone directory, it pays to check each one by eye. Then recheck it. Then check it again.

The Terrible Twos: I want those two, too. I want those too, two. Spell check thinks both these sentences are sterling examples of the English language at its finest. Don't confuse "too" and "two."

They're, There, Their: This gruesome trio likes to slip past spell check under the cover of darkness, although grammar check sometimes highlights a sentence like, "There cars are on the road" as incorrect.

Contractions: It helps to keep your possessives and your contractions straight. "Its" and "it's" are a point of confusion for many, as is "who's" and "whose," and "you're" and "your." If it has an apostrophe, it's a contraction. Without one, it's a possessive—i.e., it belongs to someone.

Then and Than: Then he did this, because he'd rather do this than that. The latter compares two values; the first is a part of speech that signifies time moving along.

THE INEVITABLE FOOTNOTE

Spell check is vital for many people who, for one reason or another, have trouble with certain words (your humble narrator among them). It wants to help you out: the problems only start when you use it as an excuse to avoid the necessary reread.

MAXIM 38

KEEP A PAPER NOTEBOOK.

A PAPER NOTEBOOK holds a handful of advantages over a laptop or tablet for the intellectual on the move. It requires no electricity. It bends and squeezes into tight spaces. You don't have to turn it on to jot a reminder. (Have you ever said to a friend with a smartphone, "Let's do lunch next Tuesday," and then waited while your friend got out the device, turned it on, found the necessary calendar app, waited for it to launch, and pecked in the details of your lunch date? A real convenience, right?) Like dogs, notebooks grow to reflect the personality of their owners, although only one of those two will react kindly if you try to write on it.

Indeed, your notebook is up for pretty much anything: you can scribble on its pages with any type of pen or pencil, in whatever direction you please, and then switch to doodling in the margins (and lest you knock the importance of the doodle, remember that Leonardo da Vinci's notebook sketches of helicopters and tanks predated the real machines by hundreds of years). Said notebook is ideal for lists, and the hasty scrawling of overheard quotes. You can paste in cuttings from book reviews and articles or, if you're my creepy next-door neighbor, endless magazine photos of a semi-naked Megan Fox. There's a reason why the notebook remains the favored companion of intellectuals everywhere: it's perhaps the most versatile way to record those invaluable ideas (and other bits) before they slip away for good.

THEORY INTO PRACTICE

Most people have very particular preferences when it comes to a choice of notebook. Ultimately, whichever one makes you feel most comfortable is best.

The Spiral Bound: As a piece of grade-school nostalgia, you can't beat the spiral-bound notebook, with its durable cover and the ability to easily tear out pages. Other intellectuals might wonder if you're feeling sentimental about your school years. (Also in this category: black-and-white composition books.)

The Little Black Book: Moleskine and similar brands offer these small notebooks, usually with an option of a handsome black cover. Their compact size makes them ultra-portable, and some offer small pouches on the inside cover for carrying additional papers. Possible downside: everyone will think you use one for storing paramours' phone numbers. (Depending on your point of view, this may be a side benefit.)

The Swag: Companies often like to give out branded notebooks for free. On occasion they're actually high quality, with splash-resistant covers and fine binding. If you can deal with an enormous corporate logo on the cover, you can't beat the price.

THE INEVITABLE FOOTNOTE

Unlike keeping a document on a computer, which you can forever preserve by e-mailing a copy to yourself or printing out several, a notebook's contents are vulnerable to twists of fate. A spilled cup of coffee or bottle of water will smear its pages into illegibility and delete those precious written gems forever. Fido can enact the student cliché about the dog eating homework, and tear your notebook to shreds. Or you could simply lose it in a coffee shop. Should the worst happen, you will be forced to piece together your previous notes from scratch, with questionable success.

If you have a great idea, it often pays to transcribe it into backup mediums—such as an electronic document—as quickly as possible. Never trust that your maniac neighbor *won't* accidentally set fire to his tiny actress shrine, taking out your apartment and notebooks in the process.

MAXIM 39

REMAIN SLIGHTLY WARY OF
TECHNOLOGY.

IN PAST CENTURIES, most intellectuals needed only a few simple tools of the trade: pen and paper, a few coins for postage, and a flat surface on which to write. Whether an author, playwright, theorist, or merely a clerk who aspired to become one of the aforementioned, those tools presented a low barrier to entry.

Then typewriters came into popular use. The machines spared aching eyes from chicken-scratch handwriting. If you learned to type quickly, you could compose multiple pages an hour without copious ink stains or wrist fatigue. For every writer who defiantly stuck with a pen as his or her primary means of expression, it seemed another two or three joined Team Underwood.

A few decades ago, computers entered the mix. They transformed deleting and editing into a fast and largely paper-free process, although some would argue it made writers more careless. You could save hundreds of documents or images on a disc, e-mail them around the world, and scream in agony as, mere minutes later, an editor shredded your work via instant messaging. The Internet grew to contain millions of texts and facts, accelerating the pace of research.

For all of technology's substantial benefits, however, it also created some thorny issues. It tempts the intellectual to place too much faith in automated tools like spell check (see Maxim 37). It distracts with gee-whiz features and games. The web remains a breeding ground for sloppy analysis and plagiarism.

An intellectual shouldn't necessarily abstain from technology, but a healthy skepticism can spare you headaches. Question how any shiny piece of hardware or software can benefit your life and work.

THEORY INTO PRACTICE

Novelist Cormac McCarthy, whose accolades range from the Pulitzer Prize to the National Book Award, relied for decades on an Olivetti Lettera 32 typewriter. When the machine wore down, he put it up for auction (where it sold for more than a quarter-million dollars), with the proceeds donated to a nonprofit research institution. Did he buy a shiny laptop as its replacement? No. With his iron faith in the old ways, McCarthy set forth with silver in one aged hand and with it purchased yet another Olivetti Lettera 32.

Some may argue that McCarthy is a Luddite, or someone who disdains modern technology. That could be the case, but he also clearly knows which tool best serves his needs. In similar fashion, when confronted with some new piece of hardware guaranteed to make your work smoother, faster, better—ask yourself, will this really serve to advance my work? Or am I being lured by those sleek graphics and glowing keyboard, this premium sound system?

When in doubt, if only for the sake of your own wallet, err on the side of McCarthy. Remind yourself that simple tools have created much of the world's finest intellectual work.

THE INEVITABLE FOOTNOTE

Some intellectuals depend wholeheartedly on the latest technology in order to express their ideas. Scientists will endlessly petition their labs for the most cutting-edge equipment. Many artists employ next-generation tools to help craft their visions; take the sculptor Federico Díaz, who required robots to build his *Geometric Death Frequency—141*, a giant installation featuring nearly a half-million plastic balls arranged in a giant wave. And yes, a percentage of writers will forever need the guiding hand of spell check to produce readable documents.

MAXIM 40

PREPARE YOURSELF FOR
FACE-TO-FACE MEETINGS.

THANKS TO TECHNOLOGY meant to make life simpler, becoming a hermit is easier than ever. Someone armed with e-mail, texting, and a web browser bookmarked with laundry-delivery and Thai takeout places is someone who never needs to leave the apartment again. Whether or not this is a boon for productivity is an open question. Would Dostoyevsky, trapped at his desk by yet another pulverizing Russian winter, have written more if he could summon some firewood and food with a few mouse clicks? Or would easy access to online poker have distracted him from mining further into his spiritual torment?

For any intellectual involved in a truly crunchy mental endeavor, the need for space and "thinking time" can become intense. Many require total silence in which to contemplate and compose. A few retreat to cabins amidst quaint wilderness, miles from interferences like friends toting six-packs.

Technology allows you to maintain that isolation. Communication by e-mail or video conferencing is flexible and easy. However, the duties of modern life soon require everyone, not just the hardcore hermit scholars, to emerge from their spiderholes for a little face time. In order to make those meetings as quick and smooth as possible (you have work to do, after all— *real* work, not sitting around and jabbering), it pays to prepare ahead of time.

THEORY INTO PRACTICE

No intellectual can escape meetings. Artists' agents and dealers demand the intellectual's presence on occasion. Designers and computer programmers need to present their work to their backers. Academics have endless faculty reviews.

Set a specific time for the meeting: Stick to it. If the other participants need information from you beforehand, make sure they receive it well in advance.

Presentation: No matter how brilliant the ideas you demonstrate before your audience, meeting etiquette demands that you appear in at least somewhat presentable form. That means shirts free of hot-sauce stains.

Set goals: With e-mail, you have hours or days to compose a multi-paragraph response to a query. Unfortunately, you don't have that same luxury of time in a face-to-face: the longer you sit there, silently puzzling over the right *bon mot*, the more uncomfortable you're likely to make everyone else at the table.

To minimize that awkwardness, diagram your goals for the meeting before you enter the room. That will help you clarify your thinking and prevent the conversation from drifting down unexpected tributaries. E-mail (or otherwise share) those goals with the other participants beforehand, to guarantee everyone has the same vision for the meeting.

Follow-up: Afterward, send an e-mail or message recounting the meeting, along with the outcomes as you understood them.

THE INEVITABLE FOOTNOTE

Sometimes arranging a face-to-face meeting proves impossible. Under those circumstances, e-mail and phones are acceptable substitutes for sitting down together. If the latter, prepare your meeting goals as you would for an in-person gathering.

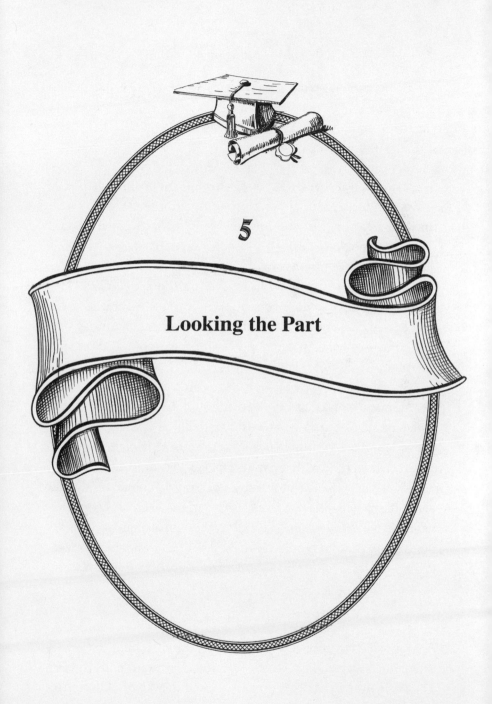

5

Looking the Part

DECLINE A PIPE OR MONOCLE
AS AN ACCESSORY.

STALKING A FLEA MARKET one fine afternoon, you stumble across a small cardboard box containing a monocle and beautiful calabash pipe, for the low-low price of one dollar. Could these become your next great eccentricity? Seized by whimsy, you purchase both items and take them home.

Once back in your humble abode, you slip the monocle over your left eye and pop the pipe-stem in your mouth. The accessories look faintly ridiculous when combined with your modern-day shirt and jeans. Nonetheless, you decide to head back outdoors in your new garb.

Passersby shoot you odd looks. You could live with that, if only the monocle worked as intended: every time you squint to read newspaper headlines and street signs, the little glass piece threatens to slip from your eye-socket. You manage to light the pipe, and the noxious clouds of smoke make you an instant pariah. Suitably embarrassed, you stumble back inside to hide for the rest of the day, having learned a key lesson: an intellectual's eccentricities can take many forms, but wearing certain antiques—whether pipes, monocles, or bonnets—makes you look less like a vintage-loving sage, and more like a time traveler horribly out of place.

THEORY INTO PRACTICE

A monocle was once the coolest intellectual fashion accessory ever—for duel-hungry, castle-owning Bavarian counts circa 1898. In much the same way, a pipe was a favored accoutrement for study and contemplation—for a London detective at the height of the Victorian era, with a roommate who didn't mind the clouds of fragrant smoke. Such items are firmly relics of another time, and wearing them can force perceptions of you as trying far too hard to imitate a mental titan of the old school.

In this spirit, any number of antique items fall into this wide category of accessories to avoid: swords, animal pelts, any suit tailored between the years 1980 and 1987 (particularly if it includes shoulder pads suitable for an NFL linebacker), elaborate lace fans from the Victorian era, riding crops (at least in public), old-style bonnets, those black-stem cigarette holders from the 1920s, canes with animal's heads carved into the handles, and whalebone corsets. Also stovepipe hats, unless you want people on the street to ask whether you're headed to an Abraham Lincoln lookalike contest.

THE INEVITABLE FOOTNOTE

Certain venues and groups encourage wearable artifacts. Recent years have seen a surge in popularity for steampunk, a subculture that combines the best (or stuffiest, depending on your point of view) of Victorian-era accessories with modern technology. Adherents to this fad take contemporary objects such as cell phones and modify them with brass and other nineteenth-century detailing, in order to give them the appearance of something H.G. Wells might have invented in his spare time while buzzed on absinthe. Your own antique accessories, modified slightly, will blend perfectly with those carried by the steampunk crowd.

Should you break down and purchase a pipe and monocle, any society of Sherlock Holmes aficionados will provide you the opportunity to use those ornaments in a safe environment without fear of scorn.

MAXIM 42

ALWAYS CARRY A JACKET.

IN HIS BOOK *The Hitchhiker's Guide to the Galaxy*, Douglas Adams states that the most useful accessory for intergalactic adventuring is, in fact, a towel. In addition to soaking up water, it can double as a blanket, a sail, a distress signal, and a weapon in hand-to-hand combat.

Adams's book is fiction, and not wholly because half its characters are space aliens: the most necessary fashion item in the inhabited universe—at least when it comes to intellectuals—is actually the jacket.

Like Adams's towels, jackets boast a practical side, serving as an effective pillow for penniless poets and playwrights crashing on a bench or a friend's couch. Intellectuals with lots of notebooks and other carrying items appreciate the typical jacket's variety of pockets.

On a broader scale, a jacket (depending on its cut and color) instantly formalizes your wardrobe. Shrug it on over a T-shirt, and you blend in, in most professional situations. At the same time, the jacket can add a touch of class at more casual events, although a pinstriped one will make you look a little out of place at a thrash-metal concert. (Yes, I have tested this theory personally.) No intellectual wants their clothing to overshadow their words and ideas, and so a jacket becomes the great equalizer—sparing you from showing up underdressed, but removable at informal moments.

THEORY INTO PRACTICE

Your choice of jacket is a personal one, but pay attention to the material: wool on a hot and humid day leaves you sweating worse than a drug mule at a customs checkpoint. A nylon or light cotton jacket in winter will provide zero protection against the elements, ensuring your transformation into a meat popsicle if you spend too much time in the open air.

Pockets are another essential element in the intellectual's jacket. If you're not carrying a bag, your outerwear must carry the combined burden of phone, wallet, notebook, pens, a slim paperback for idle moments, scraps of paper with hastily scrawled notes and addresses, random business cards and interesting bookmarks, a backup pen, a backup pen to the backup pen, documents or letters in need of your attention, and your choice of nicotine- or sugar-delivery system. A jacket at its best is your portable lair, with the added benefit of being stylish, so long as you make certain your pocketed materials don't create outsized lumps. Is that a copy of Breton's *Manifestoes of Surrealism* in your pocket, or are you just happy to see me?

THE INEVITABLE FOOTNOTE

A jacket isn't ideal for every situation. Wearing one to the beach on a blazing-hot summer day, for example, is just odd—unless, of course, you've established the constant wearing of a jacket as one of your core eccentricities.

MAXIM 43

WEAR BLACK FOR ANY OCCASION.

BLACK IS THE IDEAL COLOR for any intellectual's wardrobe. It hides stains. It suits for nearly any occasion, whether a coffee-shop literary reading or a funeral (at only one of those events can you wear shorts, however). Best of all, wearing it allows you to devote the effort and brainpower normally reserved for matching your clothes to . . . pretty much anything else.

If you try to move two objects into the same space, one will displace the other. Dunk a rubber ball in a full glass of water, and an equivalent mass of *aqua* will splash onto the table. Wearing all black works on a similar principle, by displacing the possibility of wearing something that contradicts the intellectual way of life. To wit:

T-shirts with corny slogans: In particular, from drinking establishments known for any of the following: body-shot specials, karaoke, bartenders dancing on the bar at least once an hour, cocktails with more umbrellas than a swath of vacation beach, or the hottest wings east of the Mississippi.

White suits: Intellectuals rarely double as pimps.

Anything with a corporate symbol: You were born with four limbs and a working cerebellum. You have vocal cords, and hands for manipulating the world around you. You have thoughts, and feelings, and dreams, and fears. You know what all those things make you? Not a billboard for a product.

Clothing with a *Star Wars* theme: Yes, you loved the movies, once upon a time. And then the second trilogy went and murdered those memories. It's time to let go.

Camouflage: Unless you're planning on setting this book down, gathering a few of your buddies who have nothing to do this weekend, growing a beard in honor of *El Maximo*, and invading a small corrupt country with the aim of overthrowing the government and handing power back to the people, there is precious little reason to wear camouflage. That is, unless you're a hunter in the woods. With a bow and arrow. In which case, you're probably having a little trouble holding this book anyway.

THEORY INTO PRACTICE

Wearing black is a simple maxim to follow. You may face criticism from people who take pride in wearing colors and patterns. You could find yourself swatting back at snarky questions like, "Who died?" If you tell them that black clothing is best for hiding stains, they will almost certainly retreat a few anxious steps. Better to say that you're attending an evening event, such as an art gallery opening, where everybody dresses like a raven.

THE INEVITABLE FOOTNOTE

Wearing all black to a wedding is generally frowned upon. You will be most likely forced to sit in the rearmost pew, where you can complete the image of the outsider misanthrope by sipping from a small flask and offering ironic commentary on the happy couple.

MAXIM 44

EMBRACE YOUR FACIAL HAIR.

ACCORDING TO GUINNESS WORLD RECORDS, one Sarwan Singh is the proud owner of the world's longest beard, at seven feet nine inches in length.

The only question is, how many years will that record stand? In university bars and hipster concert halls across this fine nation, a significant percentage of men seem to have decided, as if by group vote, to grow beards so large and gnarly that their lower jaws appear under assault by a grizzly cub. While these spiritual children of ZZ Top are perhaps an extreme example of recent trends in facial hair, there's no denying the urge to cultivate the bristles that grips nearly every man on occasion.

By letting their facial follicles sprout unimpeded, the intellectual emphasizes how their mental concerns far outweigh the need to maintain a clean-shaven appearance. This applies to both men and women, and it doubles as a significant time-saver: women needn't worry about the painful process of dealing with "upper lip hair" (as estheticians so delicately term female moustaches), nor pluck and wax their eyebrows into unnatural configurations. Men no longer need to face the razor every morning, with the inevitable cuts and bumps that result.

As an added bonus, facial hair lets intellectuals emulate some of the famous fuzz of yesteryear. The popularity of their theories might wax and wane, their greatest works might end up in history's Remainder Bin, but you can count on some of history's most famous intellects to boast the best in stubble.

THEORY INTO PRACTICE

A few of those intellects, in fact, serve as pretty good role models for cultivating facial hair of your own. A sampling of namesake looks:

The Freud: Sigmund Freud, father of psychoanalysis, sported a well-trimmed classic beard. This style suggests someone reserved, yet unafraid to break out the cigars and ask you about that dream involving a Canadian Mountie and a goat.

The Kahlo: The Mexican painter Frida Kahlo's self-portraits depict her faint moustache. It's a distinctive feature, one that highlights her determination to use what others might damn as flaws in order to create totally honest pieces of art. You may have the self-possession to grow one yourself.

The Thoreau: Henry David Thoreau grew a wiry thicket on the underside of his chin. It's a mildly eccentric look, hinting at wildness without ever really embracing it. Sort of like how Thoreau, seeking the transcendence that comes with communing directly with nature, isolated himself in a cabin amid Walden Pond's pristine woods—a short walk from his family's house and regular home-cooked meals.

The Marx: Karl Marx's beard was really more of a lion's mane. Like the socialist revolution, it harbored a burning desire to spread to new territory.

The Nietzsche: Friedrich Nietzsche rocked an enormous thundercloud of a moustache. Only the strongest barbers, armed with the hardiest shears, could trim those curls.

The Pushkin: As a style, large sideburns suffer from a bit of an identity crisis. In the nineteenth century, politicians and playwrights enjoyed growing muttonchops of prodigious length. That helped make sideburns seem prim and old-fashioned. Elvis and James Dean did their best to reverse this stodgy image, with their sideburns hinting at wild-and-crazy rebelliousness. Yet the poet

Alexander Pushkin boasted sideburns that played to both sides of the debate: somehow feral-looking despite their trim, prominent but understated within the context of the face.

THE INEVITABLE FOOTNOTE

A few professions preclude facial hair: scientists who need to wear specialized respirators as part of their research in toxic or oxygen-free environments, executives at corporations whose cultures frown at enormous beards, and a handful of others. Make sure your own circumstances permit you to mimic Freud or Pushkin before you start letting that stubble run wild.

MAXIM 45

DISCARD THE BACKPACK FOR
A BAG OR BRIEFCASE.

Whoever invented the backpack did the world a considerable service. Two shoulder straps bound to a sturdy bag enable you to carry massive loads over long distances in relative comfort. An internal- or external-frame pack, filled with necessities and a few tools, proves essential when navigating through a vast wilderness filled with animals only too happy to convert you into a tasty, protein-packed morsel.

There's only one little problem: you're an intellectual. Hiking through the wilderness simply isn't part of the standard job description. Nor is looking like a tenth grader on the way to homeroom. In the name of projecting a mature and scholarly air, the time has come to upgrade to either a shoulder bag or a briefcase.

THEORY INTO PRACTICE

The bag (sometimes known as the satchel or messenger bag) suggests its bearer is the bohemian type, unafraid to be mistaken for a designer or artiste. A comfortable shoulder strap is a must, along with enough pockets and dividers (in the right configurations) to ensure your belongings stay in their right place. The bag should be large and flexible enough to accommodate a laptop or tablet: a sizable model will prevent male intellectuals from being accused of carrying a "man purse," an item that few have the style and self-assurance to carry without looking totally ridiculous.

The briefcase offers its owner a more formal look. It hints that you're a lawyer or businessperson, ferrying documents of considerable importance. For intellectuals who belong to neither profession—and want to give the impression that they care nothing about status symbols—the ideal briefcase is suitably scuffed and stained, its surface rugged yet somehow charming, like Clint Eastwood's face. As with the shoulder bag, make sure the briefcase is large enough to carry your electronics of choice with enough room left over for papers and other necessities.

The portfolio is an option for those who only carry around a few documents at a time. Handle-free and small enough to tout under the arm, it remains the lightweight alternative to bags and cases, but lacks their pockets and ability to accommodate larger loads.

THE INEVITABLE FOOTNOTE

Notable intellectuals, including Bruce Chatwin and Barry Lopez, made careers out of life at civilization's rugged edge. If you choose to follow in their footsteps toward world's end, a backpack will serve as a more suitable companion than a shoulder bag or a portfolio. Remember to bring bug spray: in addition to offering glimpses of nature at its most transcendent, the wilderness includes mosquitoes the size of F-16 fighter jets.

MAXIM 46

REFUSE TO BE ASHAMED
OF YOUR VEHICLE.

IF YOU WANT TO OVERCOMPENSATE for your shortcomings (real or imagined) and tap your bank accounts to the last shiny penny, you can't do better than an absurdly expensive super-car. Owning a six-cylinder beast with a hand-stitched calf-leather interior might soothe the insecure soul, but it won't miraculously boost your driving skills: every so often, someone will spend the equivalent of a McMansion on the Ferrari of their dreams, only to discover too late the engineers weren't kidding about terms like "racecar precision," or the ability to zoom from zero to 60 mph in four seconds. By then, the absurdly expensive vehicle has plowed sideways into a delivery truck, tearing off the rear bumper—for maximum psychic trauma, think of that damage as cost-equivalent to a year's tuition at a decent university.

Unless you make a living as a professional racer who enjoys transforming every minor errand into the Indy 500 ("It's good for the road skills, dear; they need to stay finely tuned") or a getaway driver with a self-destructive urge for an easily identifiable vehicle, then there's pretty much one reason to own a pricey set of wheels: ego. And given how the intellectual's ego is linked solely to the contents of his or her mind (at least in theory), there's little need for such toys. Your decrepit old ride is a symbol of intellectual pride, a way of telling the world—or maybe just the mall parking lot—that you place more emphasis on tricking out your mind than your wheels.

THEORY INTO PRACTICE

So absorbed in the life of the mind is the intellectual, in fact, that he or she can pilot any sort of vehicle from Point A to Point B with no loss in social standing. A battered one-speed bike in a purplish color best described as "bruise," perhaps with a large flag poking out the back? Your typical office drone will never live down riding something like that to work. Placing a dedicated intellectual on the seat, on the other hand, transforms that two-wheeled horror into a token of personal whimsy, yet another sign (along with the thoroughly eccentric shirt) that a certain someone has let their thoughts drift into the higher realms.

The same principle applies to cars—not that most intellectual professions pay enough to purchase a Maserati or a Bentley. Your secondhand sedan with its crunched-up backside and tailpipe farting smoke violates enough clean-air laws to give the Environmental Protection Agency a collective heart attack, and that's okay. Your have far bigger problems to deal with, like picking apart the universe's deepest secrets or finding a way to condense the geopolitical hatred of the last century into a stanza of epic power. When in doubt, remember: your car's not crappy—it's *bohemian*.

THE INEVITABLE FOOTNOTE

A few scholars and writers specialize in automobiles and other vehicles. They're exempt from this maxim, insofar as their choice in wheels reflects their professional life. A gearhead puttering around in a junker is sort of like a self-professed wine connoisseur caught drinking from a box of cheap plonk: sad.

MAXIM 47

REMAIN UNCOSTUMED,
EVEN ON HALLOWEEN.

ONE FINE SUMMER AFTERNOON, marching across Brooklyn's Prospect Park for a wine-fueled picnic with a group of economists, I came across a peculiar sight: a dozen adult men in full armor, locked in combat with swords and clubs. A moment later I realized both armor and weaponry were made of painted foam. The combatants took great lunging swings at one another, roaring with medieval vigor whenever a "blade" connected (so very softly) against an opponent's head.

Everyone else in the park seemed either amused, horrified, or some combination of the two. Not that it stopped them from taking pictures with their phones.

Historical enthusiasts, lovers of fantasy novels, and those who want to keep other bus riders at a safe distance occasionally indulge in wearing costumes. If you mapped those groups on a Venn diagram, they would overlap nicely with the circle marked "intellectual": today's teenage Renaissance Faire aficionado has a higher-than-average chance of becoming tomorrow's preeminent Renaissance scholar.

Certain venues and events welcome participants stomping around dressed like Joan of Arc, a werewolf, or a werewolf Joan of Arc. These include Ye Olde Faire off Route 128, in that field behind the fried-chicken place. Outside such "safe" zones, costumed heroes will elicit a less-than-enthusiastic reaction from most bystanders. Conversations become strained; the costumed one is regarded, warily, as a potential escapee from the local asylum. Long-winded explanations about your interest in all aspects of European life circa 1643 will not alleviate the awkwardness. Nor will deploying the foam sword.

If you're not headed to the Ren Faire, leave the costume at home.

THEORY INTO PRACTICE

The question inevitably arises, every year, over the permissibility of costumes on Halloween. The answer is no, unless the costume in question is something understated along the lines of a pair of horns grafted to the forehead.

The reasoning here is fairly straightforward: so many adults use Halloween as an excuse to loose their repressed inner freak, which apparently involves dressing up like Heath Ledger in *The Dark Knight* and running outside fully intent on drunken destruction, or until a police officer gives them a stern look, whichever comes first. As thousands of amateur videos can attest, this wilding-out leads to idiocy that nobody wants to admit or revisit come morning.

The release-the-freak impulse runs counter to the intellectual ethos. Can you picture French existentialist Jean-Paul Sartre, one of the leading lights of twentieth-century philosophical thought, sprinting down a nighttime street with a plastic cup of cheap beer in each hand, bellowing through his devil mask about, quote, getting his drink on? I think *not*.

THE INEVITABLE FOOTNOTE

Actors are the obvious exception to this particular maxim, especially those who appear in costume dramas. A subset of method actors insists on taking their historical characters—including the clothes and accent—off the set and into the real world, which doubtlessly excites their assistants beyond belief. The difference between those actors and your average Ren Faire player, of course, is that the former is paid to personify that bygone era, effectively immunizing them from criticism. People have done far worse for a paycheck.

RESIST THE TEMPTATION
TO SHOW OFF YOUR PHONE.

IT WAS BUT A FEW SHORT YEARS AGO that phones had a sole function: making calls. Then the devices evolved from plastic bricks bolted to your kitchen wall, to slightly smaller plastic bricks you slipped into a pocket, to slim panes of glass that love it when you touch them in the right places, not to sound creepy or anything. These days your high-end "smartphone" offers the ability to answer e-mail, flick through friends' postings on your social network, hurl angry birds across a video-game landscape, edit documents, tweet a Gandhi quote, check your position on a map, and, when occasion demands, actually place a call.

Walking down a typical urban street, you might see half the passersby fixated on their stylish polycarbonate rectangle, tapping away at the screen with the blazing dexterity of a schoolgirl on speed.

As with any trend or fad, this burgeoning interest in cellphones-on-steroids has kicked off a social arms race. Attendees at parties will whip out the latest smartphone, expecting coos of awe. They passionately defend their choice of brand, as if they, and not an army of sweatshop workers, were the one who put the device together piece by piece. The ultimate irony, of course, is that people ten years from now will look back on our technology and say, with a rueful laugh, "How primitive."

The intellectual is human, and therefore capable of succumbing to the herd mentality. Indeed, surrounded by people enthusing about their phones, the temptation to join them can become overpowering. This is before the intellectual remembers that his or her self-image depends on many things, but not on an appliance you hold in your hand—no matter how shiny and small the latter.

THEORY INTO PRACTICE

To devote a portion of your ego to a phone is a fool's game, unless you want your ego crushed nine months down the line when a new generation makes your precious gizmo look like a '58 Edsel at a Formula 1 race. The intellectual simply refuses to play that game, and leaves the phone in their pocket.

THE INEVITABLE FOOTNOTE

Modern smartphones can easily run programs whose hardware requirements would have melted down a full-sized desktop fifteen years ago. In turn, that has kicked off a new market for apps and small games, lucrative enough to attract some pretty big brains with an aptitude for coding. If you're a programmer or software developer piecing together a game you hope will prove more successful than "Angry Birds" (you plan to call it "Flying Pigs"), or an app that can deliver every play and poem Shakespeare ever wrote to your screen (complete with index and supporting documents), then carrying around the latest and greatest phone is a matter of necessity: you need to test your creation, show it off to friends and potential investors, and use it liberally in public in order to attract attention. Some developers will even resort to carrying multiple devices, with an eye to guaranteeing the app runs well on every platform available.

MAXIM 49

KNOW THE NAMES OF CERTAIN DESIGNERS.

YOU CAN RATTLE OFF THE SPEED OF LIGHT to the mile-per-second, recite pi to the twentieth digit, quote Dante in Italian, and take pride in a library overflowing with books and art. While embracing the life of the mind offers an excuse for avoiding fads, it might lead you into thinking that you can sidestep all knowledge of design, especially if you've established your own style (which hopefully does not involve wearing a cape).

But design is as much a part of the human endeavor as physics, mathematics, or literature. Ever since the first primitive humans skinned a pelt, draped it over their shoulders, thought it might look better tied around the waist, decided it wouldn't match the face-paint, and then headed out to kill an animal whose fur better matched the rest of their gear—well, let's just say there's always been a desire for looking good.

Anthropology aside, design is a defining element of culture, and thus it behooves you to know some of its leading lights. These designers compelled whole generations to think more deeply about the image they present to the world.

THEORY INTO PRACTICE

A few of the more iconic ones from the past few decades, to get you started:

Giorgio Armani: Enormously influential Italian menswear designer, famous for forty years' worth of fine tailoring. Fun fact: he designed the wardrobe for Brian De Palma's film *The Untouchables*.

Coco Chanel: The French fashion genius, founder of the Chanel brand, active for much of the mid-twentieth century and so massively influential her name is instantly familiar even to those people whose idea of fashion is a (relatively) clean T-shirt and a pair of jeans.

Alexander McQueen: This British fashioner merged the primness of British bespoke tailoring with a dark-yet-whimsical sensibility. His retrospective at the Metropolitan Museum of Art in New York City attracted lines with hours-long waits.

Philippe Starck: A massively influential French designer specializing in common household items such as furnishings, giving each a unique spin (he's managed to make external hard drives and lemon squeezers look almost impossibly chic).

Frank Lloyd Wright: Arguably the most famous architect and interior planner of the past century (he certainly has name recognition that surpasses others in the field), Wright created Fallingwater and other iconic structures, emphasizing geometric shapes and harmony with the surrounding environment.

THE INEVITABLE FOOTNOTE

Just as a physicist doesn't necessarily need to learn a thing about poetry, you're not duty-bound to learn the ins and outs of designers. Our brains store only so much information. Nonetheless, knowing your Armani from your McQueen can help make you a well-rounded generalist of the old school.

As with famous painters, if you don't know a particular designer, don't bullshit: people who know clothing and building design tend to be rabid about it.

MAXIM 50

USE ANY WRITING INSTRUMENT THAT SUITS YOUR FANCY.

ON THE DAILY LIST of things to which you contribute significant thought, your choice of writing instrument probably ranks way down there, alongside such burning concerns as, "I wonder if it will rain next week," or "How many movies did Lee Marvin make?" If you need a pen, you find one nearby and use it to scrawl your signature on whatever piece of paper demands your John Hancock. It rarely matters if the instrument in question is a Bic, a curiously misplaced Montblanc, or a cheap blue-inker with "Ricky's Chicken & Gas Emporium" stamped on the side.

This is the wrong way to look at it. Your choice of writing instrument can be meaningful. Many intellectuals claim an attachment to their writing instruments. Some feel as if they can't compose without a favorite brand of pen or pencil in hand. Quentin Tarantino supposedly wrote the first draft of the screenplay for *Reservoir Dogs* in felt-tip. John Steinbeck won the Pulitzer Prize and the Nobel Prize for Literature with works originally written in pencil. Those tools got the job done.

But which tool will work for you? Just because a particular instrument worked for Tarantino or Steinbeck doesn't mean it will inspire your own writing. For a subset of intellectuals, though, a certain pen becomes part of their "signature," so to speak, along with their eccentricity and the books they choose to leave on their most prominent shelf.

THEORY INTO PRACTICE

Congratulations, you've decided to adopt a particular kind of writing instrument. Now you have decisions to make:

Ink or Pencil: With apologies to Steinbeck, a pencil can prove annoying. You need to sharpen one far more often than a typical pen runs out of ink, especially if the tip keeps breaking, and graphite has a nasty tendency to rub out or fade over time.

The Style: Felt-tip or ballpoint or gel? The only answer is whichever one makes you feel most comfortable.

The Feel: If you feel uncertain about a specific writing instrument, take it for a test run. Does it feel comfortable in your hand? Does it mesh with your style of handwriting, flowing over the paper in a way that seems effortless? If a pen doesn't feel natural, it probably shouldn't become your signature device.

And remember: always carry a spare.

THE INEVITABLE FOOTNOTE

A quill pen requires (a) the flight feather of a large bird, (b) a bottle of ink, and (c) a special knife for paring the quill. It served the multitudes well in the years before the invention of the modern pen, but composing with one takes time and tends to leave inkblots. Setting up your ink bottle and knife also takes far longer than simply uncapping a Bic. Spare the geese and embrace more modern technology.

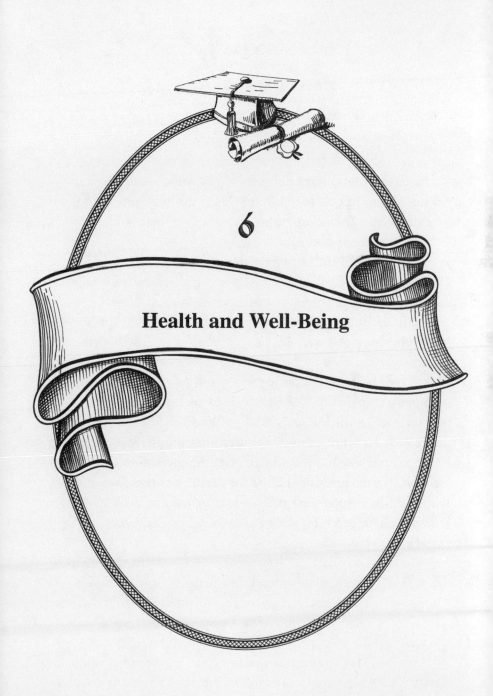

6

Health and Well-Being

MAXIM 51

BECOME A FOODIE LIKE
A ROMAN EMPEROR.

THE ROMAN EMPERORS did nothing by half-measures. Vitellius, whose reign in C.E. lasted barely eight months, proved a spectacular failure on most fronts but one: the man knew how to throw together a dinner.

According to the historian Suetonius, Vitellius created a certain dish that combined "the livers of charfish, the brains of pheasants and peacocks, with the tongues of flamingos and the entrails of lampreys." That was one of many exotic spreads the emperor arranged on a nightly basis. By the time his enemies came to assassinate him, he was probably too stuffed to run.

Gifted with near-infinite money and power, most of Rome's emperors partied harder than a load of rock stars on a Vegas binge weekend. The only reason that Vitellius, Commodus, Nero, or any other imperial miscreants didn't drive a Bentley into a hotel pool at the climax of a cocaine-fueled bender was that Rome fell centuries before the creation of the internal combustion engine or hard drugs. This decadent lifestyle eclipses their well-earned reputations as foodies, or enthusiasts of food and cooking.

By contrast, most intellectuals neglect to focus their considerable mental energies on food. In the midst of study and work, a typical diet might feature little more than a grilled-cheese sandwich, a handful of microwave popcorn, or a fast-food heart attack in a greasy paper bag.

But like music, science, literature, and mathematics, the culinary arts are supremely worthy of the intellectual's attention. Cooking blends chemistry, history, and biology into a tasty package. Many chefs double as public intellectuals of the highest order, writing books and driving discussion of how food molds a society. The intellectual who seeks to build a balanced larder of knowledge would do well to embrace his inner Roman emperor, and familiarize himself with food and the art of cooking—whether or not his own culinary attempts go up in smoke a disconcerting amount of the time.

THEORY INTO PRACTICE

Some books to help broaden your culinary knowledge:

The Omnivore's Dilemma: Michael Pollan is a culinary intellectual whose books, including this impressive tome, explore what exactly it means to eat: how our collective decisions about food impact the natural world around us, whether "organic" is truly better, and even the mysterious ingredients found in Chicken McNuggets. Another work by him, *In Defense of Food*, boils his dining philosophy down to a simple maxim: "Eat food. Not too much. Mostly plants."

The Way to Cook: For decades Julia Child helped open American eyes and mouths to the possibilities of more sophisticated cooking (*The Way to Cook* is just one of her magnum opuses). Her recipes range widely, from soufflés to complexities involving lamb, with realistic steps for preparing them (unlike some cookbooks that won't be mentioned here).

Joy of Cooking: This hefty cookbook by Irma Rombauer and Marion Rombauer Becker has served as a kitchen bible for generations of chefs. Its comprehensive pages feature recipes from stuffed boar's head to coconut macaroons.

Heat: Essayist Bill Buford's narrative of his adventures in the restaurant industry features captivating digressions into culinary topics such as pasta-making and butchering.

Whether or not you plunge fully into the foodie lifestyle, knowing more about what goes into your daily meals can encourage you to eat better, which in turn could boost your longevity. Most Roman emperors never had the chance to demonstrate that a good diet adds years to your life: the tyrant lifestyle is fun and games, but sooner or later someone always draws a sword on you.

THE INEVITABLE FOOTNOTE

When it comes to culinary literature, ignore those tell-alls where a famous chef devotes hundreds of pages to shredding his or her restaurant rivals. These narratives prove entertaining, but they often lack the cultural details craved by foodie intellectuals.

MAXIM 52

EXERCISE TO BOOST YOUR BRAIN.

BEFORE WE BREAK OUT the rusty shibboleth about your typical intellectual loving exercise about as much as a housecat enjoys ice-cold baths, consider the scholars who defined themselves with truly daring displays of physical prowess. Take Sir Richard Burton, the British explorer and author (among other roles) famous in literary circles for his multivolume translation of the *The Book of the Thousand Nights and One Night*, better known by its compressed title *The Arabian Nights*. In addition to that notable work, his bibliography includes an armful of travelogues, which required journeying through harsh places filled with people whose idea of a warm greeting was a hurled javelin. No wonder he was an expert swordsman.

Compared to that, how could anyone complain about taking a break from work to walk around the block a time or two? It comes with roughly 100 percent less chance of grisly death, unless you happen to live in a lion preserve.

Regular exercise burns body fat, improves sleep and energy levels, lowers blood pressure, and tones your "muscles" into muscles. The benefits for the brain include a reduction in stress, boosts in the brain's levels of soothing serotonin and dopamine, and possible improvements in learning and memory retention. Exercise makes the brain work better, and intellectuals want their brains functioning at an optimum level.

THEORY INTO PRACTICE

If you like an activity, you're more inclined to repeat it. Some people enjoy jogging or basketball, and mark off a few mornings or evenings per week to do so. Others choose fun sports with fewer adherents, such as handball. For those who need more motivation to head outside in shorts, imagine boasting to your more scholarly friends about your latest endeavor, and the incredible progress you've made; to that end, you can engage in sports with a certain intellectual cachet, including sailing (a favorite of the Romantics, with mixed results), fencing (in addition to Burton, Karl Marx was also a fan), or running long distances (made famous by the Greeks).

Make sure to set reasonable goals, especially when just starting out. Nobody starts off capable of running a marathon or lifting the equivalent of a Volkswagen. Keeping a record of your daily or weekly activity can prove encouraging: many runners, for example, maintain a logbook of running times, mile splits, people passed, and so on. (The intellectuals with a mind for numbers and spreadsheets use this data to plot their future progress.) Joining an activity group or hiring a trainer also spurs beginners into regular exercise.

THE INEVITABLE FOOTNOTE

It's okay to sacrifice your regularly scheduled exercise time to massive projects and "crunch periods," so long as you make a point to resume once the chaos has subsided. Avoid the impulse to double-book intellectual activities along with physical exertion—your colleagues won't like it if the only time they can discuss a project with you is on the basketball court.

SLEEP BEFORE YOU REACH
THE BREAKING POINT.

THE BUSY INTELLECTUAL, pushed to the edge of mental endurance by work, will often mutter, "I'll sleep when I'm dead." Whether an Ivory Tower academic faced with thirty pages of research paper to write by dawn, or a popular author straining for a metaphor that perfectly illustrates how the glue holding the civilized world together is the liberal deployment of bullshit, the need for sleep is often treated as an insidious enemy.

In order to stave off downy sleep, death's counterfeit, the harried thinker will drink tea and coffee by the gallon, swallow pills loaded with questionable chemicals, blast music loud enough to set the dogs howling across the street, and struggle to keep his or her eyes open by sheer willpower.

The lack of sleep leads to physical exhaustion (and heightened sensitivity to pain and temperature), failures in hand-eye coordination, and judgment and memory issues. You mean to type, "These truths are self-evident" but the words on the screen read, "Thez truthes are sefevident . . ." because your eyes no longer deliver proper signals to the brain. In the name of producing better ideas, making the right creative connections, and not burning a hole in your stomach with that twentieth cup of dark roast, you need shut-eye.

THEORY INTO PRACTICE

A paper or project constructed over a series of weeks, with much thought and care, will almost always beat one thrown together at the climax of an all-nighter, unless the all-night scholar is a once-a-generation genius who succeeds *despite* the lack of sleep. (For some reason, that concept never really imprints with college students.) Plan your projects so that you don't have to go into sleep deficit to finish them. Follow these additional tips to help you get some much-needed pillow time:

- Stop work an hour before you hit the sack, in order to give your brain time to gear down.
- Stop ingesting stimulants like caffeine a few hours before bed, to prevent you from tossing and turning once under the covers.
- Resist bringing a notebook, laptop, or tablet with you into the bedroom, where it will pose too much of a temptation to work (or watch *The Wire*) into the night.
- Avoid heavy meals and alcohol close to bedtime, both of which can disrupt your sleep patterns.
- Exercising during the day can help with sleep, but exercise within a few hours of lying down often proves counterproductive.

THE INEVITABLE FOOTNOTE

For reasons beyond your control, a deadline can sometimes appear so suddenly that sleep proves impossible. In those cases, boil up a pot of strong coffee and prepare to dig in for the night. Remember to catch up on sleep afterward.

MAXIM 54

MODERATE YOUR CAFFEINE INTAKE.

CAFFEINE IS ONE of the intellectual's most valuable tools. Whether delivered via coffee, tea, soda, chocolate, tablets, gum, or those energy drinks that taste like a fruit bat vomited into a bottle of seltzer, this stimulant has proven the friend of many a scholar with a need to rise and grind. Because caffeine in most forms is cheap and unregulated, you can consume it until your central nervous system hums like a tuning fork.

Maybe you should cut back from eight cups of coffee a day, a well-meaning friend will advise. To which your over-caffeinated self will inevitably offer a reasonable, nuanced reply: "Whatdo youmeanstopdrinkingcoffeeifIdothatI'll*die*."

As with so many substances, the caffeine addict eventually builds a tolerance to its effects. They start drinking more and more coffee or tea or soda, aching for that buzz. The addiction builds, and they begin forsaking brightly lit, jazz-infused coffee shops with four-dollar mocha lattes for those dingy little delis whose coffee urns were last cleaned during the Kennedy administration. The latter's one-dollar coffee is good for the wallet, perhaps, but awful for the stomach lining and your hands' ability to hold still.

At that point, your most diehard caffeine fanatic often decides to cut back, perhaps out of the realization that they now speak at roughly two hundred words a minute. Caffeine is the best friend of many a hardworking intellectual, but it can quickly become an enemy—making you miserable and, far worse, killing your productivity—unless you moderate your intake.

THEORY INTO PRACTICE

One to three cups of tea or coffee a day is considered somewhat normal. Twelve cups a day is a mite excessive, something everyone around you will realize the next time you grip someone's collar and yammer for them to talk faster.

If you decide to cut back, weaning yourself off caffeine can prove difficult. For heavy users, symptoms of cold-turkey withdrawal include insomnia, irritability, difficulty concentrating, and headaches. In other words, you become the life of the party.

For those looking to take a moderated "step down" approach, some researchers recommend subtracting a half-cup to a cup per day from your daily load. Although coffee purists would blanch at the thought, substituting decaf can help fulfill the psychological needs of your routine while keeping caffeine ingestion in check. In the interim, those dreaded withdrawal symptoms might creep into your life. Grit your teeth, smile, and recognize that they'll pass with time.

THE INEVITABLE FOOTNOTE

Faced with a hard deadline or a week of back-to-back-to-back final exams? Drink the caffeine you need, and worry about the aftereffects later. Sometimes a racecar driver needs to risk blowing out his engine in order to win.

MAXIM 55

USE PODCASTS FOR ULTIMATE MULTITASKING.

POSSIBLE HICCUPS in the space-time continuum aside, the average day contains 1440 minutes, or 86,400 seconds. That always seems like ample time to cross every item off your to-do list, with a couple hours to spare for reading.

The universe always laughs at your plans, though, and for the sadistic thrill of it decides to throw in a traffic jam or unexpected office crisis. Or maybe you simply find yourself transfixed by an old episode of *Seinfeld*. (The hyper-intellectual part of your brain will attempt to justify the latter by trying to analyze the show's use of comedy motifs from the Clinton era, but deep down you're really waiting to see how Jerry will screw over George this time.) Whatever the distractions, they burn away the minutes to midnight, leaving you with a long list of unfinished business.

In order to sidestep this daily time-crunch, you might embrace multitasking. But that only works under certain circumstances. You can drive and eat, although steering down a Los Angeles freeway while pouring a sugar packet into your open cup of boiling-hot coffee is an easy way to qualify for the Darwin Awards. You can't sleep and read—generations of intellectuals have made heroic attempts to overcome fatigue and, for their efforts, earned a bruise from their foreheads hitting the desk. Neglecting food or exercise works for a little while, but sooner or later your body makes you pay. So where's that leave you, options-wise?

Fortunately, a large number of activities mix well with listening. Podcasts, along with audio books, are often your best way to save time while polishing those intellectual credentials (or navigating rush-hour traffic).

THEORY INTO PRACTICE

Modern technology, which desires only to fulfill your every need (including, you know, those *special* needs), offers a growing list of devices that can speak to you in soothing tones, for your listening pleasure and relaxation. That is, unless you download one of those audio books that features Samuel L. Jackson as the voice of God, promising to deliver a biblical ass-kicking upon your unworthy self, in which case it's more like listening terror.

Audio books are perhaps the ultimate tool of the harried intellectual. The ability to jog while listening to a trained actor read Tolstoy's *War and Peace* is a boon in terms of efficiency.

Then come podcasts, or audio and video programs you can download to your mobile device on an episode-by-episode basis. Podcasts offer the chance to learn a skill, hear a lecture on a new topic, or pick up a few choice phrases in another language.

THE INEVITABLE FOOTNOTE

Our listening comprehension has limits, as does our ability to switch focus between two (or more) targets of attention. Driving down the highway, in the midst of listening to *War and Peace*, you can just as easily miss the exit *and* fail to hear a major plot point. When in doubt, reserve your audio book or podcast for those times when your tasks at hand require significantly less diligence, like making breakfast or working out on a stationary bike.

MAXIM 56

NEVER USE DRUGS AND ALCOHOL TO ENHANCE CREATIVITY—THEY DON'T.

THERE'S A WIDESPREAD MYTH that drugs and alcohol boost creativity, as if downing a whole bottle of scotch will somehow free the inhibitions and allow that masterpiece to pour out of you.

Instances of artists pairing mind-altering substances with their work extend back at least as far as the poet Samuel Taylor Coleridge, who once opined that his half-completed "Kubla Khan" (which begins with the oft-repeated lines, "In Xanadu did Kubla Khan/ A stately pleasure dome decree") had its genesis "in a sort of Reverie brought on by two grains of opium, taken to check a dysentery, at a Farm House between Porlock & Linton . . . in the fall of the year, 1797."

The Romantics, of which Coleridge was one, weren't exactly known for their pious lifestyles (more on this later in Maxim 64: "Learn to recite Romantic-era poetry on cue"), and their fame attracted a wide variety of imitators whose substance intake was only matched by the breathtaking awfulness of their poetry.

In subsequent years, other artists perpetuated—however unintentionally—that link between drugs, alcohol, and inspiration. Edgar Allan Poe, Ernest Hemingway, Miles Davis, and many others tried to quiet their demons with their vice of choice. But no scientific study has ever drawn a causal link between ingesting a particular chemical and the ability to create a guitar solo or monologue for the ages. To the contrary, the only thing scientifically proven about most drugs is that they wear down your system and, eventually, kill you.

THEORY INTO PRACTICE

Part of the issue is a general uncertainty over the source of creativity. Why can some people craft immortal works of art, while others seem barely capable of making it through the day without accidentally driving their car through a plate-glass window? What gave a young Einstein a front-row mental seat to the universe's secrets, and not his colleagues at the Bern patent office? Numerous studies over the years have sought to parse whether the creative inclination is primarily biological (i.e., you're born with it) or something that can be learned. The jury's still out.

Nonetheless, certain habits distinguish the world's more successful creators. They tend to work like beasts, performing an action again and again and again until it meets their exacting specifications. Writers and musicians in particular are famous for their ability to pick a chorus or a sentence to death. Visual artists train for years in order to paint like Caravaggio.

In addition to dedication, innate talent also plays a role. "She's just got the gift," says the proud parent, as her eight-year-old prodigy plays a near-flawless piece on the violin.

Did Coleridge experience an opium-fueled vision so powerful it inspired one of the notable poems of the nineteenth century? Perhaps. Yet it took his talent and skill as a poet to make that hallucination a reality for generations of readers. Likewise, William Faulkner might have hit the bottle on a regular basis for his own reasons, but legend suggests that when it came time to write he never touched a drop.

THE INEVITABLE FOOTNOTE

There are no exceptions to this maxim. Nobody ever found creativity or talent waiting at the bottom of a bottle.

MAXIM 57

CONSUME THESE FOODS
FOR THOUGHT-FUEL.

THE ADULT HUMAN BRAIN weighs approximately three pounds and contains some 100 billion nerve cells. From the brain stem, the command center for heartbeat and other vital activities, to the frontal lobes, responsible for higher functions such as language and judgment, every structure plays a role in making us who we are.

Like any complex engine, the brain craves fuel. It needs glucose to operate on an hourly basis, along with the right combination of nutrients in order to maintain nerve function. Nutritionists recommend a diet high in fruits, vegetables, and whole grains, with consumption of fats and processed foods kept to a minimum. Too much of the latter—i.e., trying to subsist for too long on vending-machine snacks and soda—and your mind slows to a sickly crawl. The following foods are just a few that can help you keep thinking your best for years to come.

THEORY INTO PRACTICE

Whole Grains and Starchy Vegetables: Whole-wheat bread and pasta and vegetables such as potatoes and beans contain complex carbohydrates, which your body breaks down in a more orderly manner than the simple carbohydrates found in many processed foods (including soda and candy). This fuels your brain without giving you wild ups and downs in energy.

Wild Salmon: Omega-3 fatty acids, found in wild salmon, could potentially help stave off dementia, depression, and Alzheimer's disease. Walnuts and cod liver oil (among other sources) also boast high levels of Omega-3.

Blueberries: Studies have shown that lab rats served a diet supplemented with blueberries enjoy certain cognitive benefits, including improved memory. Granted, you test a rat's memory by running it through a maze, not exactly the sort of obstacle a human faces in the course of an average day (unless you're Jack Torrance, Jack Nicholson's character in *The Shining*, in which case you have far larger problems). Nonetheless, a handful of blueberries on a regular basis could present longer-term benefits.

Dark Chocolate: Current research suggests that the antioxidants in dark chocolate (the kind extremely high in cacao) target free radicals that damage cells. However, the sugar and fat in chocolate make it a food to consume in moderation.

Avocado: Loaded with "good" monounsaturated fat, potassium, and other nutrients essential to a healthy body (and mind), avocados place high on the list of best brain foods.

THE INEVITABLE FOOTNOTE

Every other month, it seems a new study touts the health benefits (or drawbacks) of yet another type of food. These sometimes spark health trends, where everyone on the street suddenly appears determined to suck down a gallon of pomegranate juice every day. Whether or not embracing these trends will indeed prolong your life an extra twenty years—or merely provide a note of irony to next Tuesday's fatal accident involving a rampaging moose—keep in mind that, when it comes to body and brain, a well-balanced diet is ultimately what's most important.

MAXIM 58

TAKE FREQUENT BREAKS TO BOOST YOUR PRODUCTIVITY.

FEW OF THE WORLD'S GREATEST WORKS were composed in twenty-minute bursts amidst juggling chores and errands. Sooner or later (emphasis on "later," given the typical intellectual's predilection for blowing deadlines), the mental titan faced with an epic project will need to brew a pot of coffee or tea, switch off the phone, order some food, and arrange their workspace for an hours-long work session.

At this point, the temptation arises to labor in one long, uninterrupted stretch. Even if it means drinking coffee until your teeth grind. Even if your friends and family start leaving messages on your voice mail, wondering if you're still among the living. But sitting there for hours—nose buried in voluminous texts, pen scratching its way through page after page of your notebook, fingers tap-tap-tapping away at the keyboard—has one unavoidable side effect: you become fatigued. Your thoughts slow to half-speed. Your frustration over minor details builds into a mushroom cloud of rage, frying your analytical abilities.

The experienced intellectual knows that taking frequent breaks isn't a sign of laziness or inability to complete the task at hand; rather, short siestas can refresh your mind and ultimately raise your productivity.

THEORY INTO PRACTICE

"Work smarter, not harder" is one of those catchphrases that appear on motivational posters hanging in the office kitchen, tolerated only because nobody can muster the righteous indignation against corporate-speak necessary to tear it down. As with a startling number of overused expressions, though, it contains a sizable grain of truth. Ramming your head against a brick wall in order to break it down will result in a piercing headache, if you're lucky, and little damage to the brick. Contrast that with actually taking the time to puzzle over the problem, finding a sledgehammer, and figuring out where to hit the wall so it collapses in a pile of shards and dust: much easier, with less pain, thanks to a bit of brainwork.

Part of working smarter involves taking breaks, which studies suggest has a restorative effect on your mind. Some years ago, a Cornell University study found that computer users who took short rests "were 13 percent more accurate on average in their work than coworkers who were not reminded," according to the school's press release. It's not a stretch to imagine the same truth holds for anyone using his or her mind to make headway on a project: take a couple-minutes break once every hour or so, and watch as you outpace someone who insists on staying glued to her chair.

THE INEVITABLE FOOTNOTE

If you're a procrastinator, a fifteen-minute break can seamlessly transform into a two-hour television marathon, a long walk, or an exciting opportunity to do laundry. Setting a defined "rest period" (complete with ringing alarm) can stop you from drifting too far away from the work at hand.

MAXIM 59

SHUN DRINKING AT THE RECEPTION
OR BOOK READING.

EVENT PLANNERS tasked with filling their receptions and book readings with crowds of eager attendees—and who need to do so without access to a Famous Person to appear as the headliner—have evolved one surefire method of ensuring success:

Offer an open bar, and stock it with pretty much anything. Wine remains a perpetual favorite at intellectual events. Whether cheap *vino* in a box, chemically indistinguishable from engine cleaner, or the good stuff from some quasi-mythic vineyard where each grape is ritually massaged and crushed beneath the delicate feet of virgins—people will line up to drink it down. And hopefully stick around for whomever speaks that night.

However, heavy drinking at the reception or reading can sometimes prove disastrous. A few too many glasses of wine, and the most reserved attendees start believing they're the second coming of Richard Pryor: they launch into a joke, except they keep backtracking to the part when the horse first walks in the bar, and ten minutes later they're still babbling to a group of listeners nearly willing to chew off their own arms to escape, coyote-style.

Don't be that sort of event drinker. Inebriated rants (and questionable behavior) have a funny way of undermining an intellectual's public persona as an erudite speaker and reasoned thinker. Plus, you want to foster a reputation based on your ideas, not gossip about how you tried to leave the party with the buffet table's decorative ice sculpture in your arms.

THEORY INTO PRACTICE

Fortunately, the solution isn't particularly complicated: avoid the temptation to overindulge in any alcohol offered at an event. Set a limit; nurse water or a soda in between glasses of the harder stuff; and remember that photos of the night's events will almost certainly end up on Facebook. Just because an event involves a Pulitzer Prize winner reading from his latest work of genius doesn't mean you shouldn't employ the same rules for surviving a hard-drinking night in a sketchy dive bar.

Should you require motivation to keep that imbibing in check, remember this: although your average human being has a tendency to forget everything from their spouse's name to their own phone number, they possess the stunning ability to forever recall others' *faux pas* at public events. If you've ever gotten drunk at an academic talk, for the next twenty years your friends and colleagues (and enemies) will inevitably remind you of that sloshed evening, and in the most embarrassing ways. "Hey!" they'll shout in the middle of a dinner party. "Remember the time you got so trashed on chardonnay you vomited on Noam Chomsky's shoes?" At that point, you might seriously consider committing harakiri on the spot.

THE INEVITABLE FOOTNOTE

Some receptions and readings require a more liberal ingestion of alcohol, if only for your own survival. Unless you're a medieval studies person, for example, a four-hour talk about the evolution of language in the context of twelfth-century English poetry is endurable only with the assistance of a good buzz. (Interminable awards ceremonies also fall into this category, unless you're a presenter for such an event.)

MAXIM 60

UNLEASH YOUR CRO-MAGNON SELF WITH GRILLING.

In the minds of some, the term "intellectual" is synonymous with "wimp" or "pushover." This is one of those unfortunate stereotypes that refuses to die, and a particularly unfair one: an affinity for knowledge is never exclusive from the ability to endure adversity, whether hiking across Death Valley with little water or suffering Justin Bieber music for twenty hours straight with no ill effects.

However, there exists one straightforward way for the intellectual to demonstrate their lack of fear in the face of fire, smoke, sharp objects, and complicated directions: grilling.

Hold on a second, you say. If the intellectual in question is carnivorously inclined, couldn't they better demonstrate their fortitude by actually killing their own food? Perhaps, but hunting is often inconvenient for the city- or suburbia-dweller: it requires purchasing a firearm or other type of killing tool, finding some forest, crouching in the damp brush for hours or days (attracting a nasty cough and a million bloodsucking insects in the process), engaging in a terrifying inner dialogue over whether you have what it takes to whack Bambi's mother, and finally driving to the nearest general store, where you can purchase several pounds of mystery meat from a backwoods Rambo who uses a bow and arrow to dispatch his prey with steely efficiency.

Nearly everybody, on the other hand, can grill. An afternoon of roaring fire, fragrant smoke, and pretending you dominate the food chain will do much to persuade everyone that you're more than an activity-fearing bookworm.

THEORY INTO PRACTICE

Bookstores and cooking-supply outlets offer dozens of volumes on the delicate art of grilling on hot coals or gas. Those books focus on the finer points of sauces and handling different kinds of meat and vegetables. In the meantime, here are a few tips for averting total disaster:

Prep: Clean the grill beforehand. This prevents the food from sticking, which can screw with your presentation (you'll still need an expert team of food-preparers and photographers to make that steak look anything like the photo in your cookbook). Spice and marinate your meat or vegetables at least an hour before you actually begin to grill.

Don't Undercook: Invest in a meat thermometer. Undercooked meat can lead to food poisoning, and that can kill you, and that would be bad.

Keep Watch: More than one intrepid griller has wandered away from the fire to refill a drink and returned to find his beautiful steaks reduced to lumps of smoking charcoal, or else part of the porch dissolving into a gaudy flame. Lesson: keep an eye on a lit grill.

Burn, Baby, Burn: Gas grills often include a temperature gauge. For charcoal grills, most cookbooks recommend gauging the heat by sticking your open palm a few inches over the coals. If you can hold it there for five seconds without needing to pull away, that's low heat. Three or four seconds is medium heat, two seconds is high heat, and one second means you're a masochist.

Follow the Recipe: Cookbook-writing chefs are the intellectuals and experts of their field. Trust them in the same way you'd trust a physicist to instruct you in the finer points of dark matter.

THE INEVITABLE FOOTNOTE

If outdoor cooking and fire don't persuade everyone that you're the toughest intellectual they ever met, you'll have to resort to Plan B: a weekend camping trip.

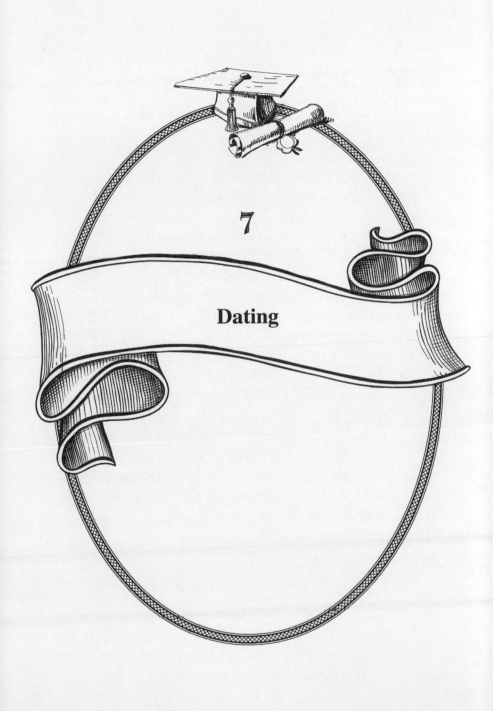

7

Dating

PERUSE THESE HUNTING GROUNDS FOR YOUR FELLOW INTELLECTUALS.

Just as birds may flash plumage or wail in ways irresistible to members of the opposite sex, budding scholars and weary academics alike engage in specific actions to signal their suitability as mates. Carrying around a book in hopes of sparking conversation is such a time-honored tactic—although one must be careful to pick the right title. Kundera's *The Unbearable Lightness of Being* is a solid choice, because many intellectuals have a warm opinion of it: you start discussing Tomas and Sabina, and fifteen minutes later you have a coffee date. However, some books are a little too obvious as props for romantic chatter: D.H. Lawrence's *Lady Chatterley's Lover* falls into this latter category.

In the same vein, some eccentricities and modes of dress can serve as the intellectual's romantic calling card. A lobster on a leash, to take a cue from Nerval, will drive someone to ask the inevitable question, which in turn could lead to what the online dating sites so ambiguously refer to as "something more."

If you're looking for another intellectual with whom to swap theories, feelings, and the occasional cold virus, the following places could serve you well in your hunt.

THEORY INTO PRACTICE

Libraries: A noted gathering place of intellectuals since the ancient Library of Alexandria. **Pros:** No shortage of prospective intellectual mates, who could find charming your attempts at wooing via handwritten note. **Cons:** The no-talking rule, enforced by the librarian's Glare of Doom, requires you to work fast when asking for a later meet-up.

Coffee Shops: Your local coffee shop serves double-duty as an office or study lounge for many intellectuals, raising your chances of finding a suitable date while ordering your daily cup of caffeine. **Pros:** As with libraries, people make their corner hangout a part of their daily or weekly routine, giving you multiple chances to flash the art book you bought for that very purpose. **Cons:** The combination of caffeine and nervousness can turn you into a babbling, sweaty wreck.

University Bars: Across the street from the University of Chicago's main campus sits a dive called Jimmy's, whose only difference from your standard-issue watering hole is the set of encyclopedias that supposedly live behind the bar, for settling scholarly disputes. That's exactly the sort of detail separating university bars from regular ones, and why intellectuals looking to unwind gravitate toward the former. (Although it must be said, with regard to Jimmy's, that I never saw anyone use the encyclopedias in question during my many, many hours of "studying" in the corner.) **Pros:** Alcohol, dim light prove forgiving. **Cons:** The jukebox blasting Modest Mouse's "Float On" for the twentieth time in a row can drown out your titillating conversation about D.H. Lawrence.

Lectures and Talks: These draw intellectuals like moths to a bug light. **Pros:** Ample fodder for opening lines: "So, what'd you think of the lecture?" **Cons:** The majority of people attend these events to learn, not to flirt.

THE INEVITABLE FOOTNOTE

Many of these places double as the intellectual's home (or office) away from home. If the object of your affection rejects your advance, don't press your case—otherwise you'll create an uncomfortable atmosphere, and probably need to find another café to hang out in.

MAXIM 62

MAKE DINNER FUN,
NOT AN IQ ARMS RACE.

IT'S TEMPTING for intellectuals to show off their depth of knowledge. "So after the Battle of Marathon *(huff, puff)*, legend says the Athenians sent this runner named Pheidippides *(cough)* back to Athens to announce victory," you might tell the rest of your running group, as you collectively pass mile five of your weekly route. "And he made it *(wheeze, huff)* back, shouted that the Greeks had won, and died. Doesn't that put jogging *(cough)* in perspective?"

Your running group, meanwhile, is too busy gasping for air to appreciate the history lesson. Yet in this and many other situations, you feel the need to share a piece of relevant knowledge. And why not? The intellectual's purpose is to parcel out knowledge to the world at large, no?

Yes—except when it comes to dating. Whether or not you've decided to engage Maxim 61 ("Peruse these hunting grounds for your fellow intellectuals") and chase after your fellow thinkers, you can benefit by refraining from that long monologue (no matter how well-rehearsed) about the possibility of neutrinos surpassing the speed of light, or how the restaurant's lighting reminds you of Ad Reinhardt's *Abstract Painting*.

For dates not inclined to intellectual pursuits, those types of discussion topics may quickly alienate them, and they will never take your calls again. If your companion is a fellow intellectual, there's an equally high likelihood your flagrant display of knowledge will kick off the dreaded IQ arms race.

Very few intellectuals, confronted with someone trying to show off the size of their brain, can take the high road and simply nod along. We are competitive animals at heart, and while that impulse has its benefits—i.e., spirited debates, intellectual rivalries that push you to refine your arguments—it also leads to verbal brawls in lieu of romantic interludes.

THEORY INTO PRACTICE

If I had to choose between a date imploded into a tussle over who's smarter and being torn apart by a pack of crazed wolves, I would probably opt for the latter as being quicker and less painful. Unlike a regular debate, which involves actual issues and points of view, the only goal of the IQ arms race is demonstrating a "superior" intelligence.

In order to do so, both sides fire off longer and ever-more-convoluted arguments or explanations, burying the original point of discussion—or rather, the excuse for the two of you to reach for increasingly esoteric bits of knowledge—beneath a metric ton of pointless verbiage.

Your date: "I just can't agree with you about *Drive*. Its camera-work and soundtrack were clearly meant to lull you into thinking the film was an homage to those '80s movies where the audience is expected to see the vigilante as a heroic figure. Then it flips, by revealing that heroic figure as a total psychopath. If you can't see that, it's probably because you've never seen the source material."

You almost say: "To the contrary, I once wrote an essay for the *Times* about how Eastwood and Bronson influenced vigilante movies. I think you might be wrong about *Drive*. The whole thing is meant to be ironic. Furthermore . . ."

You *should* say: "This soufflé is rather good, isn't it?"

You can't win. It's no fun. The date is deader than Pheidippides. Best veer the conversation onto a different track.

THE INEVITABLE FOOTNOTE

You're trapped on a bad date, with no salvation in sight. What to do? You could head to the bathroom, and text a friend to call you in ten minutes with some crisis that needs your attention (cliché). You could fake a fainting spell, but that might result in paramedics and awkwardness. Or you could launch into an endless monologue about the underlying themes of Graham Greene's *The Quiet American*, never pausing for breath. By minute ten, your date will be shuffling off to the bathroom to fake an emergency call of her own. Problem solved.

MAXIM 63

ALWAYS GROOM BEFORE
HEADING OUTSIDE.

A DAY OR TWO before the start of finals, a typical university or college library will host dozens of students in (relatively) clean clothes, smelling of soap and shampoo, their hair neatly trimmed. A week later, a sizable fraction of those students will be in those same seats, buried by books and half-written papers. Only now, having devoted every second of their lives to memorizing functional groups for that organic chemistry final, they will resemble a group of survivors from a plane crash in the Alaskan wilderness, bedraggled and wrinkled and a little (actually, more than a little) smelly. You'd almost be afraid to sit too close, lest they lunge at you for a little filet of leg.

A couple of days without a shower and a change of clean clothes inevitably leaves us not so dainty fresh. In the midst of intellectual pursuits, though, that's often the least of your concerns. Who cares if your body odor will poleax the cat at ten yards, so long as you keep an intense focus on crafting your masterwork for the ages? Beethoven was supposedly quite unkempt, and it worked for him, right?

Wrong, especially when it comes to dating. As a sign of respect for yourself, and for the person who could sit within arm's reach of you for hours, prepare to engage in a serious scrub-down.

THEORY INTO PRACTICE

Generations of engineers and designers toiled in obscurity for hundreds of years to deliver the ultimate in hot-water convenience, not to mention flushing toilets and showers. It would be insulting to deny their efforts. Flip on those taps and douse yourself down. Remember to use soap, whose proud history as a chemical compound extends back to the ancient Egyptians and beyond.

Next up, it's time for a little shaving and grooming. Yes, those rituals might force you to conform against your will to the cruel stereotypes imposed upon you by an uncaring, monolithic society. On the other hand, as proven by Europe throughout the Middle Ages, lack of widespread hygiene contributes to plague and pestilence. That's not to say that a razor and a couple of splashes of witch hazel are the only things preventing a widespread descent into contagion and terror, but cleanliness starts somewhere.

Last step: clean clothes. Some budding scholars choose to wear the same pair of jeans for months on end. Whether those jeans see the inside of a washing machine during that period is a questionable proposition, as is the likelihood of romantic company if the denim starts to smell musty. Fresh and stain-free clothing marks you as someone who pays attention to basic needs, including those of others.

Now that you're officially presentable, it's time to head out the door. Remember to take along your highly intellectual book.

THE INEVITABLE FOOTNOTE

Once you've dated someone for a little while, you can afford to ease up slightly on the grooming restrictions. By that point, they've already seen you in enough situations to deal with the appearance of a scraggly mini-beard (I call that one The Guevara), or a T-shirt maybe three days past its optimal freshness.

MAXIM 64

LEARN TO RECITE ROMANTIC-ERA POETRY ON CUE.

FOR THE MOST PART, the Romantics weren't a very romantic lot. Lord Byron, whose poetic sensibilities gave us the love-letter-ready line, "She walks in beauty, like the night," awoke on his wedding night with a piercing scream of, "Good God! I am surely in Hell!" (He was once termed "mad, bad, and dangerous to know" for a reason.) Percy Bysshe Shelley, a poet of substantial renown and husband of *Frankenstein* writer Mary Wollstonecraft Shelley, lived out years of tragedy and scandal, including the abandonment of his wife and infant child to run off with Mary. The English poet and novelist Letitia Elizabeth Landon endured rumors of affairs and illegitimate children born in secret, which may have driven her to suicide. And the Russian writer Alexander Pushkin (perennial candidate for the title of Greatest Sideburns of All Time) lost a duel and his life to his wife's alleged lover—certainly awkward for everybody involved.

In short, not exactly lifetimes brimming with flowers and chocolates. But the Romantic era, and its intellectual wild children, had little to do with what we call romantic love. America and France burned with revolution, the Industrial Age was gathering steam (so to speak), and suddenly people began questioning whether the old ways and means still applied. Poets and thinkers rushed to embrace nature and the archetype of the heroic individual, one capable of creating his or her own reality. In the process, they wrote some pretty good lines in order to express those ideas and, yes, mayhap perform a little seduction in the process.

It's the power of their language and not necessarily the lives they lived or ideas they advocated that make the Romantics so quotable two centuries later. However ironically, those quotes are incredibly effective in romantic situations, if deployed at the appropriate moment. For an intellectual, they represent the best of all worlds: capable of melting the iciest heart, while also hinting that you're incredibly well read in fine verse.

THEORY INTO PRACTICE

The Romantics weren't exactly subtle. Love poetry from other eras tries for elegant and understated, the lyrical equivalent of a quiet dinner-for-two at that one Italian restaurant in your town without neon in the window. That sort of date isn't exactly what Romantic verse had in mind. It wants to pick you up at ten in its big black car with the purring V8, and drive you at thrilling speed to that scenic roundabout, where it will play violin for you by moonlight. It will fall to its knees and worship you with joyful tears, and then wipe those tears from your feet with its hair. It will do everything those other poems cannot, and if you reject it, it will set itself on fire, because of the pain of that will soothe in comparison to the agony of losing your heart forever.

The Romantics as a whole generated a considerable body of work. In terms of poems you'd want to quote on command at the right moment, you need only a few, starting with Byron's "She Walks in Beauty":

She walks in beauty, like the night
Of cloudless climes and starry skies;
And all that's best of dark and bright
Meet in her aspect and her eyes;

There's also Shelley's "To a Lady, with a Guitar," a longer and somewhat more complex poem that boasts a kicker:

For you he only dares to crave,
For his service and his sorrow
A smile to-day, a song to-morrow.

Charlotte Turner Smith, another poet from the period, brought the Romantic obsession with nature to bear in a sonnet dedicated "to the moon." A fragment of that ode to an orbiting ball of rock, however, is easily converted to a short, sweet romantic missive:

And while I gaze, thy mild and placid light
Sheds a soft calm upon my troubled breast;

Reciting such lines can spark an atmosphere of heartfelt emotion, and deepen your bond. It can make your mate burst into laughter and ask, not unkindly, "Where'd you learn *that*?" Either outcome counts as a win.

THE INEVITABLE FOOTNOTE

At moments the Romantics' poetry pushed a little hard on the passion front. Take this selection from Byron's "Lara":

In vigilance of grief that would compel
The soul to hate for having lov'd too well.

Those lines read less like love-letter fodder and more like the motto of that weird dude in the bushes with the binoculars. Always make sure to quote appropriately.

MAXIM 65

REFRAIN FROM USING
THESE PICKUP LINES.

Do PICKUP LINES WORK? Has anyone in history ever scored off the tactful deployment of, "Hey baby, what's your sign?" or, "Bond. James Bond"? Could an infinite number of barflies, cruising an infinite number of watering holes and clubs, earn someone's phone number by saying: "I'm not the best-looking person here, but I'm the one talking to you. How about it?" (An infinite number of monkeys, clattering away on an infinite number of typewriters, would probably have a better shot at producing an error-free copy of *Hamlet* within an hour.)

There exists the slimmest chance that a clever opener, delivered with the perfect spin of self-awareness and irony, could jump-start a conversation. That quark-sized possibility, however, will blip out of existence if you lard the spiel too soon with heavy intellectual knowledge: instead of serving as a most excellent preamble for why your respective genes would mix so well, it forces any resulting conversation onto a very narrow track.

THEORY INTO PRACTICE

You spy an utterly charming individual at the local coffee shop and mosey over, feeling brave. There's just one issue: you have no opening gambit. Five feet away, mind scrambling for a phrase with more coherence than "Um, uh, um, hi," you point at the hefty psychology book in the charming individual's hand and say:

"If you ever want to talk Freud, I promise not to bring up my Oedipal complex."

Way too self-deprecating, of course, and far too creepy if true—those aside, the line is a textbook case of mixing too much intellectualism into a pickup line (if there actually existed a textbook for such things; I guess this book qualifies). Your dialogue is now trapped on a track involving neurotics and psychotherapists, from which the most commonly used exit is, "Great talking to you, but I need to go."

By that point, the only way to steer the conversation in a more positive direction—i.e., toward the securing of phone numbers, e-mail addresses, and agreements to meet for something more substantial—is to deploy the linguistic skills of Dorothy Parker, the smoothness of John F. Kennedy, the comedy chops of Louis C.K., and the luck of that one lady who holds the record for tumbling out of an airplane at thirty-three thousand feet and surviving with some broken bones. Unless you're the result of an experiment combining the genes of all those people—in which case, you're a very odd-looking individual—then it's probably in your best interest to keep that opening line free from too much intellectual heft.

You might also want to avoid any of the following:

"I'll be the smart one if you'll be the cute one."

"You don't mind parents' basements, do you?"

"I usually spend most of my time in the library. I'm trying to work on my socialization skills."

"If you want to head back to my place, I can show you some of my monographs."

THE INEVITABLE FOOTNOTE

One pickup line that always works, or at least spares you from immediate shoot-down: "Hi, my name is . . ."

MAXIM 66

LEAVE YOUR T-SHIRTS AT HOME.

IF YOU'RE AN INTELLECTUAL, chances are good you own a favorite T-shirt with an obscure pun across the front (in keeping with Maxim 9, "Tell jokes only 0.05 percent of people will understand"). It could read "Darwin is my Homeboy," or "Nietzsche" in burning-chrome lettering ripped straight from the cover of a hair-metal album.

You love this T-shirt so much, in fact, that it's tempting to wear it on a date, especially if your prospective mate is an intellectual. The logic in this action seems ironclad: you want to demonstrate that you're a fun person, utterly lacking in the anal-retentiveness or pretension sometimes associated with scholars and mental titans.

Your date will almost certainly not appreciate the T-shirt. Not even if she shares your sense of humor or taste in casual wear. The fact that you're wearing it suggests you've approached the first or second date with the same seriousness as an all-night study session on your couch. Unless your idea of a good first or second date is an all-night study session, in which case you have already earned a solid *F* in dating.

THEORY INTO PRACTICE

Of the T-shirts that deserve banishment to the wardrobe gulag before that Big Date, all boast one of the following attributes:

A Sports Logo: Unless it's the Super Bowl, and your brother is a member of a team's starting lineup, and your date takes place at a Super Bowl party. This rule can extend to a relative in the World Series, but no lesser sporting events.

A School Crest: Yes, you attended a notable (or not-so-notable) institution of higher learning. Or you want casual passersby to think you attended Harvard, despite the risk of an alumnus engaging you in conversation. T-shirts with a school name or logo serve one purpose: soaking up exercise sweat.

A Band or Movie: Depending on the band or movie ("My Life with the Thrill Kill Kult"), such a T-shirt could send a very wrong signal.

Ironic Slogans or Labels: You may end up mistaken for a hipster—and not in a cool (i.e., young Bob Dylan) sort of way.

THE INEVITABLE FOOTNOTE

On a sweltering day, a plain T-shirt is perfectly acceptable for a more casual date. That means no logos, symbols, political slogans, lyrics, or images of Han Solo.

MAXIM 67

CRAFT A TIMELESS, UPSCALE MIX-TAPE.

FIRST THINGS FIRST: the traditional mix-tape, that plastic cassette loaded with songs painstakingly copied from other sources, is dead. Compact discs and digital music pounded the nails into that particular coffin. What exists today is the "mix-tape," a term loosely applied to custom-made CDs. I feel the need to make that distinction, because otherwise I'll harbor this paranoid fantasy of opening my e-mail inbox one morning to find dozens of messages from old-school music purists, anxious to offer an etymology lesson.

When it comes to budding relationships, a mix-tape falls into the same category as a handwritten note. *I've taken the time to craft this*, it says, *because I care about you.* An intellectual might see building such a track list as an ideal opportunity to show off his or her music knowledge, and invite a similarly eclectic mix from their soon-to-be significant other. At its best, the intellectual mix-tape sparks a hum of appreciation from the recipient as they look over the songs on offer, along with the prospect of some in-depth conversation later.

Quick side tip: When making your own mix, avoid songs too obscure or depressing.

THEORY INTO PRACTICE

Nick Hornby, in his oft-quoted novel *High Fidelity*, gives some advice on arranging songs for a mix-tape:

"You've got to kick off with a corker, to hold the attention . . . and then you've got to up it a notch, or cool it a notch, and you can't have white music and black music together, unless the white sounds like the black music, and you can't have two tracks by the same artist side by side, unless you've done the whole thing in pairs and . . . oh, there are loads of rules."

Come to think of it, that wasn't helpful. Better to rely on a bit of advice from my buddy Ian, a music aficionado with a bigger album collection than a decent-sized music store, who's told me on more than one occasion: make sure the music flows. Keep any crackly lo-fi recordings a few interim songs away from the overproduced walls of sound. M. Ward's "Requiem" and Martin Sexton's "Glory Bound," with their melancholy guitars, make a fine pair beside each other. Marvin Gaye's "Got to Give It Up," smashing head-on into Marilyn Manson's cover of "Personal Jesus," do not.

There are no wrong songs for a mix-tape (to each their own). But keep in mind that after a few months, your typical pop hit starts showing its age worse than the patients in a plastic surgeon's waiting room.

THE INEVITABLE FOOTNOTE

Never make a mix-tape consisting solely of John Cage's "4'33"" on repeat. The recipient probably won't get the joke, although it might earn a smile from an intellectual with a taste in esoteric music.

MAXIM 68

OBEY STANDARD RULES OF ETIQUETTE.

I WAS FINISHING DINNER in a small restaurant across from Tokyo's Harajuku Station when I learned something very interesting: if you leave a tip after finishing your meal, the waiter will pursue you down the street afterward to return it. That would be inconceivable in the United States, where *not* leaving a tip might compel your server to give chase, albeit for completely different reasons.

Etiquette differs wildly from country to country, and sometimes within different parts of the same country. Whether tipping or bowing or removing your hat indoors, these social rules hold one thing in common: violate a major one, and others will stare at you as if a giant set of cockroach legs sprouted from your back, Kafka-style.

Many societies use etiquette as a tool for excluding outsiders: if you're spearing your main course with the wrong fork, for instance, you obviously don't belong at that table. For centuries, that alone has proven reason enough for some people—rebels, punks, those who view conformity as a straitjacket—to violate any and all social mores in their path. A number of intellectuals have joined this mutinous category, musicians and artists and authors who saw fit to swing from the chandeliers while the rest of the partygoers concentrated on uttering the right phrases in the proper order.

Other thinkers neglect etiquette out of sheer obliviousness, their minds otherwise occupied by the abstract and theoretical. On a university campus, the professor or graduate student who forgets to hold open a door or say "please" is a common occurrence, one often shrugged off by others.

But etiquette exists for reasons other than giving classical composers like Mozart something to shun and academics another venue for unintentional comedy. In prodding everyone to follow standards, such social rules smooth out some of the drama of human interaction. The intellectual who follows the rules can spend less energy and time dealing with ticked-off acquaintances, and more on thinking and work.

THEORY INTO PRACTICE

Etiquette is also essential for dating. Precious few will gravitate toward a potential mate who sneezes on his food, corrects others' grammar left and right (usually prefacing that bit of rudeness with, "I don't mean to be rude but . . ."), refuses to remove sunglasses indoors, lights cigarettes without asking permission, and tops everything off by inquiring about your annual salary.

For most people, fortunately, etiquette is something you first learned as a child: rather than having to adapt to something new, the challenge is having the presence of mind to follow (no matter how distracted your mind or how challenging the situation) the rules ingrained in you from the start.

Those raised by wolves, or who merely want a refresher in the finer points of acceptable behavior, can consult the works of Emily Post and other etiquette writers. Keep in mind that following their maxims to the letter, in our increasingly standards-relaxed world, could make you appear excessively old-fashioned, like Don Draper trapped at a grunge-rock concert. Should you decide to pursue that more stringent course, take heart in those intellectuals who, in contrast to the more rebellious sorts, embraced etiquette as a necessity of modern life (in what you might consider an irony of ironies, America's Founding Fathers—notably Benjamin Franklin, who wrote about appropriate behavior in his *Poor Richard's Almanack*—were sticklers for proper form even as they rebelled against British rule).

THE INEVITABLE FOOTNOTE

There are times when bending the rules of etiquette becomes a matter of necessity. If a party is truly awful—as in, Seventh Circle of Dante's Inferno awful—you and your date can leave before the guest of honor (once upon a time, this was a big no-no). Intellectuals may see fit to break the old rule forbidding talk of politics or religion at the dinner table, if only to free up more topics for banter. Other examples exist, although sticklers for etiquette would argue that only the more extreme circumstances would permit bending the rules.

MAXIM 69

TAKE CARE WHEN REVEALING YOUR
FAVORITE [FILL IN THE BLANK].

You're midway through a picture-perfect intellectual date, complete with a trip to the museum (thanks to Maxim 85, you do not glance at Braque's *Violin and Candlestick* and yell, "Picasso!") and a discreet bottle of wine on the marble steps afterward. The conversation features a startling lack of awkward pauses—at least until your date speaks the four little words that could scuttle your romantic evening. I call those four words the Tripwire:

"What's your favorite [fill in the blank]?"

The question comes in several exciting flavors, including movie, book, musician, and artist. Ninety-nine-point-nine percent of the time, your answer is controversy-free. That last point-oh-one percent is what risks snipping off your budding relationship at the root, depending on how you handle it.

There you are, pinned to the museum steps by the sheer magnitude of the question. You have no option but to tell the truth:

"It's, um, Bret Easton Ellis's *American Psycho*."

If you hear a metallic *ping* at this moment, that's the Tripwire. An intellectual shouldn't avoid a loaded question—that'd be a waste of a good conversation starter. However, the answer can sometimes spur a kneejerk response that, in turn, threatens to blast the conversation's positive flow to smithereens. Tell the truth but watch your footing.

THEORY INTO PRACTICE

Bret Easton Ellis, also the author of *Less Than Zero* and *Lunar Park*, has a reputation as a controversial writer. That stems largely from

American Psycho, whose Wall Street protagonist—a sick bastard named Patrick Bateman—does unlovely things to his fellow human beings with power tools. Its defenders argue that Bateman serves as a particularly vicious metaphor for conspicuous consumption. Its detractors assert the book is a misogynistic piece of crap and that people who love it are probably one bad week away from becoming serial killers themselves.

If your paramour falls into the "detractor" category, you could face a very thorny discussion and the prospect of no second date.

Movies like Peckinpah's *Straw Dogs*, along with certain musicians (Eminem springs immediately to mind) also count as Tripwires. Visual artists and philosophers more rarely fit the category, although I have a friend who refuses on principle to date anyone who enjoys Damien Hirst, whose most famous artwork is a tiger shark floating in a giant tank of formaldehyde (among other works involving preserved bits of animals).

Lying about your tastes isn't an option—dishonesty is the one thing that will kill a relationship fast. Instead, do what intellectuals do best and defend your position. Argue its merits in your most respectful manner. Project the confidence that comes from having your case already prepared in your head. And use humor: "What, you mean *American Psycho* isn't your favorite book?"

If you feel the urge to wimp out, you can position a controversial favorite as one of many: "I like Eminem but also Beethoven. It really depends on the day and how much of a homicidal mood I'm in." (That joke might be taken the wrong way.)

THE INEVITABLE FOOTNOTE

On occasion, hitting a Tripwire can enliven an otherwise dull outing. And if you've already decided to forego a second date, you can even stumble into the argument with aplomb. Confess that you love listening to Eminem while cruising lonely roads alone late at night, seeking trouble, or that a framed Hirst reproduction dominates your bathroom wall. Such revelations could help create a truly memorable evening for both of you.

MAXIM 70

TREAT YOUR EX WITH CIVILITY.

LOVE MAKES YOUR SOUL CRAWL out from its hiding place, the author and anthropologist Zora Neale Hurston once wrote. To which I can only add: breakups make it want to crawl right back in. Even relatively angst-free splits offer moments of minor heartbreak, especially the handover of stuff that formerly lived at your ex's house: the well-thumbed copy of *Gravity's Rainbow*, the feathered cap you wore at the Ren Faire last September, your boxers. The major crackups feel like your heart's been carved out with a spork.

Breakups with another intellectual are particularly aggravating. Both of you can analyze a situation to pieces, and yet all the rationality and cleverness in the world will never fix a terminally broken relationship. So you're single again, haunting that one dive bar whose eccentric jukebox offers Nick Cave and Emily Wells, puzzling over the pros and cons of online dating. And then your ex walks in, arm-in-arm with some bearded dwarf in a straw hat. Is that her rebound? Or is it true love, a kindred soul who whispers Romantic fragments into sleeping ears?

Ten minutes ago, you were sipping your beer and thinking, "I will survive." Now you're wondering whether you can pay the bartender to knock you mercifully unconscious. Whatever happens, remember: it pays to stay civil; the intellectual lets rationality and coolness rule his or her behavior, rather than the urge to implode into a twitching wreck.

THEORY INTO PRACTICE

It's simplicity itself: if the relationship ended poorly, to the point where your ex still refuses to return your box set of Kieslowski's *Decalogue* films, you treat that ex with civility whenever you meet. If it ended well, and the two of you continue to see each other as friends (or "Friends"), you treat your ex with civility whenever you meet. It may not be painless. In the former case, you may prefer a leisurely stroll across a bed of hot coals than to endure three seconds of idle chitchat—and your ex might feel the same way.

A major component of the intellectual lifestyle involves embracing mind over matter, calculation over impulse, and rationality over emotion. Granted, some of history's most famous intellectuals serve as sterling examples of how *not* to treat the ones you love, from failed marriages to barroom brawls with their best friends. We're human, and that means committing grave errors from time to time. But we can also aspire to the better angels of our nature, to quote Abe Lincoln.

Take a deep breath. Pay a compliment or two. Smile. If one of you accidentally steps on one of those landmines underneath every failed relationship, refuse to let that tip the situation into an argument. Keep smiling. Extract yourself when the timing seems natural. Resist the urge to sprint for the exit.

THE INEVITABLE FOOTNOTE

If the relationship was an abusive one, don't bother with civility—simply escape.

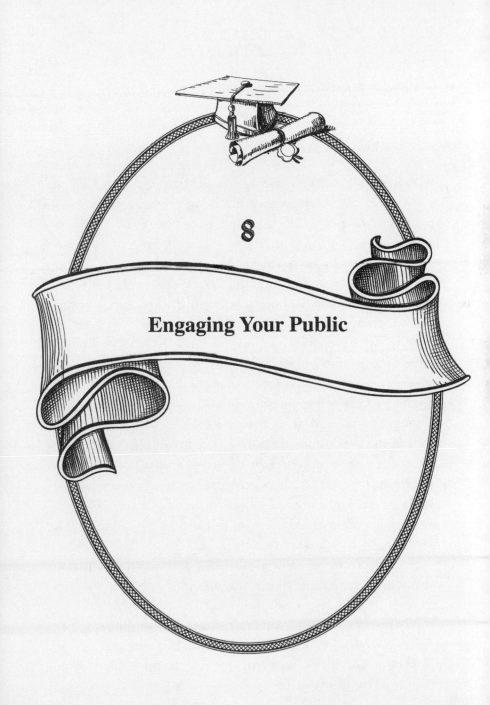

8

Engaging Your Public

MAXIM 71

EASE SLOWLY INTO DEEP CONVERSATIONS.

BELIEVE IT OR NOT, your average person prefers not to kick off an everyday discussion with a headlong plunge into a philosophical morass, especially if it happens to be early in the morning and you're blocking his access to the coffee machine.

Should you hunger for a lengthy powwow about big issues, your best option may involve gathering a selection of intellectual friends. On an otherwise boring Friday night, this nearly always proves a cheaper and more entertaining option than heading out to see whatever chases-and-explosions spectacular is playing at the local multiplex. Find an equal number of atheists and religious types, say, and place them around a table with enough stimulants and food to power an army, toss out a question like "Is there a God?" and sit back for a debate that, hopefully, won't result in the Tenth Crusade taking place in your living room.

On occasion, a profound question will grumble to life inside your head, with nary an intellectual friend in sight to help you pick it apart. Under those desperate circumstances, you may need input from a casual acquaintance or random passerby. Or maybe an earthquake just rocked your office building, spooking you and your coworkers—with whom everyday conversation usually revolves around your Keystone Kops of a local football team—into a Big Issues talk about fate and eternity.

Whatever the reason, you're on the verge of plunging into a deep conversation with someone new. For best results and everybody's comfort, make sure they're receptive to such an intellectual mind-meld.

THEORY INTO PRACTICE

Test the conversational waters with a mundane topic:

Good: "It's sure hot today, huh?"

Bad: "Whether or not you believe in climate change, you have to admit it's a terrifying concept. Think about how this place will look in fifty years, if the temperature keeps rising by however much every year. It'll be desolate, unable to grow crops, and the last survivors will have to cannibalize each other to survive. On a related note, I've been exploring nihilism lately. How do you feel about that?" Then gently probe your talking partner's knowledge level. The intellectual wrestling with an existential conundrum might try something along these lines:

"I'm really tired today. I was up late reading Camus. Have you ever read him?"

Their answer will determine whether you can plunge into more philosophical depths, or stick to wondering aloud if that nice lady in HR will fire everyone by week's end. Should the probe result in your partner shaking their head "no" or giving a disinterested grunt, you risk imploding the whole conversation if you decide to dive anyway. Like so:

"I'm really tired today. I was awake late staring at the ceiling, filled with the most perfect sense of dread. I keep thinking of this quote someone told me; they said it was from Camus: 'It is normal to give away a little of one's life in order not to lose it all.' Last night I kept wondering: have I given away enough? Or have I already lost everything?"

You will earn odd looks from your office mate, but should your probe draw some interest from that friend or colleague—then, game on.

THE INEVITABLE FOOTNOTE

Philosophical or deep conversations can sometimes erupt out of nowhere (even the least introspective are prone to occasional bouts of self-examination, although it can take a very bad week and a tanker-truck of beer). Consider these an open invitation to voice your biggest and best ideas without fear of backlash.

MAXIM 72

SAY LESS, ESPECIALLY WHEN THEY EXPECT MORE.

IN THE COURSE OF A LIFETIME, your average intellectual speaks and writes millions of words. Academics and authors in their autumn years often boast whole stacks of publications with their name printed on the cover. Their mouth opens, whether at the dinner table or a sold-out speech, and listeners expect a torrent of ideas to pour forth. Indeed, your average intellectual will want to deliver that flood, if only to justify the countless hours spent buried in texts and pondering the immensities.

The intellectual's drive to fill any given space with words, however, runs smack into the brick wall of the average listener's attention span, which, in a desperate attempt to keep pace with modern life, now clocks in at three seconds maximum on any one subject. Compare that to a few centuries ago, when humanity found four-hour symphonies and two-hour speeches the height of pulse-pounding excitement. In the present day, a twenty-minute talk on composers or playwrights is liable to send most listeners into a deep REM sleep.

With that in mind, you might hesitate to deliver that epic idea-dump for the ages. Nobody wants to clear their throat and open a reference book to the appropriate page, only to look up and find their acquaintances' eyelids drooping with preemptive boredom. But fear not: it's society's fault. Back in the Age of Enlightenment they would have reacted to your short speech on Middle Eastern politics with the buzzing enthusiasm of teenagers in a mosh pit.

Instead of the long-winded speech, you can flip expectation on its head (and snap awake your most jaded compatriots) by condensing your thoughts into a few chosen words. In these attention-deficit times, a carefully honed argument, delivered in a few key sentences, carries significant intellectual heft, precisely because it appeals to listeners trained (thanks, Internet) to give you seconds as opposed to minutes.

THEORY INTO PRACTICE

As any writer of haikus, flash fiction, and fortune cookies can tell you, it's hard work to boil down thousands of words' worth of meaning into a handful of choice phrases.

Aforethought: Thinking over your points before speaking will give you the chance to cut unnecessary scraps and fat. The upside: your audience could interpret any silences on your part as wisdom.

Cut to the Point: Edit out the preamble. Forego the introductions. Chuck the personal reminiscing. Place your thesis at the start, and take care to make it as concise as possible.

Stay Off Tangents: I once had a professor of ancient warfare who would start class by writing three topics on the board ("Greeks, Persians, Romans," for example), launch into his lecture, and promptly veer onto a side-tangent about bronze weapons or Roman siege machines. By the end of class, he would only have one (sometimes two) of the three points covered, and yet the final exam—probably the same one he'd delivered to his students, with no variation except for the date on the top, since 1987—asked questions about topics never discussed. Excessive tangents are the surest way to drift away from your main point, add word count, possibly alienate your audience, and . . . oops. I'll stop.

THE INEVITABLE FOOTNOTE

Some speaking situations remain immune to any attempts at shortening their word count: political speeches, keynote presentations, wedding toasts, and opening statements in courtroom battles. Tempting as it would be to condense an hour of talk to a simple "Thanks" or "My client was sleepwalking when he knocked off that convenience store," sometimes you need to expand a little more on the topic at hand.

MAXIM 73

REHEARSE, REWRITE, REHEARSE,
REWRITE . . .

A PERVASIVE MYTH suggests that geniuses produce their masterworks
in a finished state. That the poem came to them in a dream, beautiful and complete, or the theory somehow unspooled from their pen
without input from others. This is an excellent myth for geniuses and
artists to cultivate about themselves, because it elevates their work to
a superhuman nirvana, far beyond the hills of balled-up paper and
months of frustrated redrafting that mark most projects in progress.

The nirvana is a fantasy. The number of works requiring endless revisions and false starts far dwarfs those birthed easily into
the world. F. Scott Fitzgerald, for example, tortured *The Great
Gatsby* through a Herculean number of drafts in order to create
what many view as one of the finest novels of the past century.
Physicists and scientists and mathematicians will tinker with a
theory until it's proven or they drop dead, whichever comes first.
Your initial idea, no matter how seemingly brilliant at first, can
always use a little refinement. An intellectual always wants to craft
a clear and truthful work, one that presents his or her ideas in the
best possible light, even if it means endless revamps and tweaks.

THEORY INTO PRACTICE

I know a book editor in charge of wrangling some very big authors.
She advises them to shove the first draft of their latest book in a
drawer and keep said drawer shut for months. Her logic is straightforward: An emotional attachment to your creation can drive you
to work on it for weeks or months or years—but for all the good it

does as motivation, emotion also blinds you to the flaws. (Just ask the mother whose little snookum-wookums baby is a biker-gang enforcer with more tattoos than the California state prison system and frightening skill with a knife.) Time away from your project allows those emotions to cool, and for the details to become so unfamiliar that you can revise with a cold and analytical eye. One thing you notice when reading biographies of famous intellectuals is how they keep circling back to the same ideas, probing for new angles, sometimes until the executor of their estate pries the work from their cold, dead fingers.

A similar theory applies to public performances, such as a lecture or speech. Rehearsal (in the mirror, aloud, or before an audience of friends) presents the opportunity to strengthen the weak parts, edit for length, and adjust your cadence. Yes, some of history's greatest speeches were delivered fast and loose, the products of great emotion. But many more passed their speakers' lips only after considerable thought and enough rewrites to keep a paper mill running for a year.

THE INEVITABLE FOOTNOTE

Sometimes those numbers or words on the page become too precious: you succumb to the urge to tweak, add, delete, adjust, shorten, move sections, lengthen, and then burn the damn thing in the nearest wastebasket and start again from scratch. More than one creator has abandoned an epic project out of sheer frustration, or kept writing until the manuscript mutated into a thousand-page monster. Ralph Ellison, award-winning author of *Invisible Man* (not to be confused with H.G. Wells's book about a lunatic Brit with severe pigmentation issues) worked on his follow-up novel for decades, amassing untold pages in the process, and declined to publish until the day he died—a loss, many would argue, for American literature. Sometimes it's worth sending your project out into the world, if only so you can free your mind to move onto the next one.

MAXIM 74

CULTIVATE RIVALRIES WITH OTHER INTELLECTUALS.

NIKOLA TESLA versus Thomas Edison. Sigmund Freud battling it out with Carl Jung. Isaac Newton and Gottfried Leibniz at each other's throats. The New Atheists like Richard Dawkins and Christopher Hitchens, doing their best to shut down every religious scholar on the planet. Obi-Wan Kenobi and Darth Vader. A bitter rivalry is good for the mind, as it drives opponents to sharpen their arguments to a fine rhetorical point, while serving as great entertainment for outside observers. The world would truly be a gray and cheerless place without the willingness, on the part of its leading thinkers, to destroy their enemies' theories in the public eye—and sometimes annihilate their enemies' lives for good measure, although for history's sake everyone pretends to regret that later.

In that spirit, any budding intellectual would do well to collect at least one nemesis. However, this is more easily said than done.

THEORY INTO PRACTICE

Finding a *physical* opponent is easy: walk into the nearest bar, down one beer to dull the ensuing pain, and then pour a second on the shoes of the biggest, toughest-looking ape in the room. An intellectual adversary, on the other hand, often requires a burning theoretical issue over which to battle. Tesla and Edison differed on which type of electric current, AC or DC, was best for the world. (Insert AC/DC and "Highway to Hell" jokes here.) Freud and Jung split over theories of the unconscious mind. Newton and Leibniz (and their respective acolytes) locked horns over calculus, a burst of excitement that branch of mathematics has yet to reclaim.

If you're a scholar imprisoned in academia's Ivory Tower, your enemies usually arrive gift-wrapped. Depending on your area of study, you choose to follow this theory over that one, or learn at the feet of certain professors over others. That inevitably places you in conflict with those scholars who subscribe to other arguments. A furious publishing of monographs will ensue, followed by some bitter e-mails and perhaps an actual debate in person.

Outside of the Ivory Tower, the gentle art of making intellectual enemies is a bit more arduous. Thankfully you have the Internet, the greatest forum ever invented for verbal assault, particularly if you want it delivered by hundreds of random strangers. Step one involves starting a blog or website devoted to a controversial topic. Choose your intellectual opponents—pundits and other bloggers make good targets—and aim to hole their claims beneath the waterline (be sure to include links to their blogs or websites). Remember to keep your language clean: too much profanity and your arguments can be easily dismissed as Philistine ranting. An elegantly phrased and well-reasoned claim, however, demands one in kind. Game on.

Unless your newfound enemy kicked your dog or stole your significant other, keep your battle focused on intellectual topics instead of personal ones (more on this a bit later, in Maxim 75: "Fight every idea war honorably and well"). Remember that both sides benefit from this back-and-forth, in the form of stronger arguments and discarded ideas. (On the other hand, if they really did kick your dog, it's Darth Vader time.)

THE INEVITABLE FOOTNOTE

The hotter and more vicious the conflict, the sooner it tends to die down. That principle applies to everything from debates over God's existence to hip-hop feuds (notable exceptions include

World War II). There are few things more exhausting than constant warfare, especially when the opponents mean to draw blood. Whether you drop the issue without a word of explanation, or offer an excuse that you're "on hiatus from the public eye" while you "finish writing that book on intellectualism," sometimes the best response involves stepping away.

MAXIM 75

FIGHT EVERY IDEA WAR
HONORABLY AND WELL.

THE WORST POSSIBLE RESPONSE to an idea is total apathy. In light of
that, another intellectual launching a war of words against your idea
is perhaps the highest possible compliment. It's important, though,
to keep the battle—however intense—limited to the debate forum
or printed page; physical brawls in public places are taboo.

The distinction needs to be made, because many an intellectual war throughout the ages has spun out of control. The
cerebral arguments in those past eras generally focused on topics
such as religion and government, which have been known to
draw the strong opinion on occasion. Did some of those thinkers, sprinting for a nighttime boat and safety in another country, a hot mob on their heels, take comfort in their ideas having
such an incredible effect on others? That probably depended
on whether they ended up captured, drawn, and quartered (in
which case, the default answer is "probably not").

Take heed from their mistakes: Fight your idea wars honorably, well, and preferably without fire.

THEORY INTO PRACTICE

As discussed in Maxim 74 ("Cultivate rivalries with other intellectuals"), a conflict between two or more intellectuals offers the
chance to sharpen your rhetorical skills against opposing arguments. In the course of that sharpening, a previously well-reasoned
debate, in which both sides profess their mutual respect, will
occasionally descend into the scholarly equivalent of a Midnight

Madness demolition derby, where the contestants do their level best to smash each other to pieces.

The line is nearly always crossed when one side makes the debate personal. Equating your intellectual opponent to Charles Manson (see the war of words between authors Gore Vidal and Norman Mailer in Maxim 95: "Laugh at jokes made at your expense"), or sleeping with their spouse in order to slam home an abstract point about free will, qualify as making the situation personal.

Don't make it personal.

Should a debate verge on transforming into a grudge match, a simple apology can fix things—oftentimes, even after everyone thinks the situation has slipped past the screaming, object-tossing point of no return. It might require the first move on your part, since most people would rather lose all their possessions in an out-of-control poker game than utter "I'm sorry" with genuine emotion. An apology won't settle the underlying debate (nor should it, if both sides have good arguments to make), but it will ensure that the combatants can share space at a gathering without launching into an animalistic snarl-fest.

At the same time, the first and foremost object of the well-fought idea war is to defend your arguments. Ideas can evolve over time, fed by new information, but should always spark your passion to the point where you're willing to fight for them—or hide out in a hay cart bound for the nearest convenient coast.

THE INEVITABLE FOOTNOTE

One day, you may open your eyes and realize that, for whatever reason, your ideas are indefensible. These Road to Damascus moments often compel intellectuals to change their public views, a thorny process thick with self-doubt, former allies crying hypocrite, and other drawn-out agonies. Despite that chaos, such a switch could prove better for your conscience than fighting for ideas in which you no longer have faith.

MAXIM 76

LOSE A DEBATE GRACIOUSLY.

No MATTER HOW PERFECT your debating skills, defeat (or at least a draw) is at some point inevitable. Whether you talk yourself into a corner or your opponent offers a more compelling argument, or you spill hot coffee in your lap and cede the battlefield to run screaming from the room, you will someday lose an intellectual head-to-head.

Defeat might crush your ego to a fine paste. It may drive you to reach for the nearest bottle of something high-proof, or an antidepressant so powerful it'd make you burble "I'm cool with this, bro!" in the face of imminent nuclear Armageddon. Neither of those count as acceptable behaviors, because—say it loud and proud—defeat is inevitable. The only question is how you react to the defeat.

Some people do not react well. They kick things, which is more likely to injure the foot than the thing. They curse out their opponent. They fume, stomp, yell, cry, and do everything in their power to become a tooth-grinding annoyance to anyone in the vicinity.

In elementary school, we called these people sore losers. With the onset of maturity and a broader vocabulary, we can offer a more nuanced—nay, *wise*—term for these misguided individuals: douche bags.

And such douche bags, having let emotion override their thinking, aren't conducting themselves in particularly intellectual fashion.

THEORY INTO PRACTICE

In the context of losing a debate, Operation Do Not Be a Douche Bag is rather simple to execute.

Imagine this scenario: you're attending a dinner party well stocked with wine, food, and intellectuals with a burning need to push their opinion on the week's big political issue. The debate starts in earnest. For an hour you manage to hold your own, relying on a combination of statistics cribbed from *The New York Times* and a few ideas "borrowed" from a political blog you hope nobody else at the table reads on a regular basis.

Then your advantage starts to slip away. One of your opponents flanks you with a key fact, follows it a moment later with a vital statistic, and then administers the *coup de grâce* (that's French for "you're doomed") with a theory from a famous thinker that, yes, really puts the whole thing in perspective—just not your perspective. You sit there, hemming and hawing, as that smug bastard across the table helps himself to a triumphant glass of rosé. How to deal with this stinging loss?

Option A: Growl, "I'm still right," and refuse to say anything for the rest of the night.

Option B: Scream, "Wrong!" and pound the table like a drum.

Option C: Toss the breadknife into a nearby wall and stare wordlessly at your dinner companions until they slink from the room in shame.

Option D: Raise your own glass, nod, concede with something vague and positive ("That's certainly a good point," or "There's a lot of merit in that position") and shift the conversation as quickly as possible onto a new track. Remember to smile and, if you're the competitive type who transforms every touch football game into a bone-crushing tackle-fest, not grit your teeth with rage.

If you enjoy things like actual company at dinner, Option D is likely the best.

THE INEVITABLE FOOTNOTE

Sure, you lost the debate. Life is bleak. The soundtrack wails with mournful violins. I have one word for you: rematch. Boost your knowledge of whatever issue, bide your time, and then oh-so-subtly position yourself for Round Two. If your opponents are true intellectuals, they will accept the renewed challenge. Just don't strike out twice in a row.

MAXIM 77

BE POLITE,
IF ONLY TO SIMPLIFY YOUR LIFE.

INTELLECTUALS MAKE THEIR BIGGEST MISTAKE when they decide their massive brainpower proves them superior to other human beings. Nothing could be further from the truth. The ability to quote Romantic poetry or explain the theory of relativity will transform you into a superstar at the book-club gathering, but your lack of tire-changing skills makes you more useless than a hammer without a handle if you end up stranded by the side of the road with a blowout (unless you've followed Maxim 91: "Learn the arts of tool use and changing tires"). Meanwhile, that same guy you chided at the gathering for his ignorance of Byronic verse, well, he can swap out a flat in three minutes—and he just buzzed past you in the left lane, flipping your stranded self the one-finger salute. Different situations demand different kinds of intelligence.

In light of that, it always pays to be polite. Maybe even a little bit humble.

THEORY INTO PRACTICE

The ability to demonstrate an immense body of knowledge is the intellectual's reason for climbing out of bed in the morning (and, already absorbed in deep thought, tripping over their own shoes). Displaying your smarts in the wrong fashion, however, can quickly irritate and anger those around you:

"It sounds morbid, but whenever I hear the word 'prune' it makes me think of that Seamus Heaney poem 'Strange Fruit,' which repeatedly uses the word 'prune' as a way to describe the process of death and putrefaction and, perhaps, beatification. What, you've never heard of Heaney? He only won the Nobel Prize in Literature. Did they teach you anything in school besides basic addition? Where *did* you attend school, by the way?"

You will be shunned. Better to modulate that phrasing a bit:

"The word 'prune' reminds me of this great poem by Seamus Heaney called 'Strange Fruit.' He's one of those poets whose meaning can be a little hard to figure out, but he's totally worth reading."

The latter statement expresses a bit of humility and doesn't challenge the listener's potential ignorance of the topic at hand. It will result in your shirt staying beer-free.

If anything, politeness plays a greater role in everyday interactions, where your intellectual mind has terribly little influence over whether your food is delivered or bus arrives on schedule. Unfortunately, that fails to stop the occasional scholar on a schedule from a very public meltdown:

"What do you mean, my prosciutto-on-gluten-free isn't ready yet? I can't wait any longer. I have a talk on transcendental literature to give in half an hour. Do you have any idea how many people are waiting to hear me speak? Of course you don't. Why did I bother asking?"

Fun fact: employees from all walks of life react badly to long, verbose challenges, especially ones that call their character into question. A better response to your server raising the 'just one moment' finger:

"Okay, thanks. I'll be waiting over here."

One moment of politeness can equal an hour of screaming, with regard to your needs being met in a timely fashion. Harried servers certainly appreciate it.

THE INEVITABLE FOOTNOTE

You're in a coffee shop during the morning rush, waiting for your daily fix of caffeine with sugar, when a fellow intellectual (you can tell because of the *Tropic of Cancer* tucked under his arm) begins tearing into the barista about the status of his triple latte with foam. He refuses to back down. Even worse, he's holding up your coffee order, which should be considered grounds (pun intended) for justifiable homicide. You are absolutely within your rights to step forward and apply curtness, along with a bit of snap ("What would Henry Miller do in this situation, you think?"), in order to help resolve Latte Armageddon.

MAXIM 78

ABSTAIN FROM USING GOOGLE IN FRONT OF OTHER PEOPLE.

BEFORE THE RISE OF GOOGLE and other online search engines, it took years of effort to build a mental library of trivia and odd facts. You knew the adult human skeleton had 206 bones, or that Sir John Harrington invented the modern flush toilet, because you either read it in a book or heard about it in class. In turn, you used these little tidbits to raise your social standing at parties and other gatherings, swooping in to save conversations stalled by lack of random knowledge. If that earned you some odd looks and comments ("Gee, I had no idea that Africa was the second-largest continent"), it was a small price to pay for spreading a little information. Boosting your own ego had nothing to do with it, nope, not a bit.

Then search engines came along and ruined everything. "Hold on, I'll look it up on my phone" became the bell-toll for those intellectuals whose lives revolved around trivia night at their local watering hole, specifically the moment when they could spring above the flummoxed crowd and proclaim, "Actually, *I* know! The Nile is an estimated 4180 miles long!"

If everyone can whip out their phone and find the answer to virtually any question in less than eight seconds, then what purpose do these once-proud figures, the brains who spent untold years storing all manner of esoteric knowledge, serve the world? Absolutely none. They become yet another species doomed by the relentless march of progress, like the broad-faced potoroo or the dodo bird. For the sake of intellectuals everywhere, we cannot let that happen.

THEORY INTO PRACTICE

There is a silver lining: thanks to the widespread use of Google, producing an answer without checking a nearby screen makes you seem three times as smart (and four times as attractive to any intellectuals standing nearby). Moreover, the novelty and convenience of having a massive search engine feed everyone instant data makes the human brain seem puny by comparison, and thus relieves the pressure on you to deliver a precise answer. In that context, a ballpark figure recited off the top of your head is just as worthy as an ultra-precise, ten-digit one read off a website. You earn extra intellectualism points for questioning whether the data offered by Google is, in fact, accurate.

Don't know the answer to a certain question? Resist the impulse to scramble for the nearest keyboard; someone else at the gathering likely has the query halfway typed into a device. By following suit, you concede that humanity has forever lost the knowledge wars to our silicon-based overlords. Which is true—but nobody wants to *admit* that fact.

THE INEVITABLE FOOTNOTE

Certain situations demand that you swallow your intellectual pride and scramble back into the loving arms of the nearest search engine, which is ready to forgive you for shunning it.

Finding Directions: Whether stuck on a lonely stretch of highway with only a sketchy gas station in sight, or in an urban jungle whose residents seem to take perverse pleasure in guiding you in circles, it's time to set aside your pride and search online for directions.

Practical Math: Need to convert dollars to yen, gallons to liters, or figure out the tip on a restaurant bill? Save yourself the messy frustration of paper-napkin calculations, and rely on your phone's browser for a quick, accurate number.

Movie and Concert Times: Do they even print these on paper anymore?

MAXIM 79

PLAY IT COOL, BUT NOT COLD.

In 212 b.c., Roman troops sacked the city-state of Syracuse on the coast of Sicily. Frustrated after a two-year siege, they rampaged through the streets, slaughtering any resistance—and encountered one citizen who refused to let the apocalyptic fire and chaos ruin his workday: the renowned Greek mathematician Archimedes, whose hobbies (legend has it) included designing war machines capable of capsizing Roman warships. Archimedes was in the midst of studying a diagram when a soldier arrived with orders to bring him before General Marcus Claudius Marcellus.

"Do not disturb my circles," Archimedes supposedly said, referring to the drawing, and paid for his insolence when the soldier struck him down. That was almost certainly the stupidest mistake of the centurion's soon-to-end life, as Marcellus had asked for Archimedes unharmed.

If you believe that story (as with many tales from antiquity, it was written down well after the fact), then Archimedes became a martyr of intellectualism, for placing the mind's work ahead of all other concerns, including a sword to the back. Yet his example also suggests that perhaps obliviousness to others' emotions isn't always your best course of action.

THEORY INTO PRACTICE

Playing it cool is one thing: a little skepticism never hurts, especially when it comes to late-night infomercials and other people claiming they've found a surefire way to strike it rich with penny stocks. Moreover, the intellectual overeager to embrace a new idea is one who risks having to backtrack once the inevitable cracks appear in the initial concept.

Playing it cold is a different animal. People expect you to react when things happen, whether or not the bulk of your attention and brainpower is focused on work. Many acceptable replies exist to someone telling you that their dog died, for example, but none of them feature you saying, with an air of distraction and perhaps a little shuffling through papers, "Um, that's unfortunate. Have you seen my copy of Baudrillard's book? I'm trying to finish this project by tomorrow."

Recent years have seen a newfound focus on emotional intelligence, or the ability to perceive others' emotions while understanding and regulating your own. Various theorists have offered models for measuring emotional intelligence, with most incorporating some form of empathy as a significant element. That means taking an interest in others' concerns, accommodating requests within reason, and at least pretending to care when your city happens to be on fire.

That work in emotional intelligence aside, academics continue to argue whether increased empathy translates into concrete, real-world results. And some of history's most effective leaders have been despots, both literally and figuratively speaking. For those of us who don't run a major company or a banana republic, though, relationships with other people are ultimately all we have, which is why it's important to understand others' emotions and manage them—in addition to managing our own. It might even prevent one from being stabbed.

THE INEVITABLE FOOTNOTE

If you subscribe to the idea that emotions can cloud judgment, then coldness is often the one sure way to succeed in business pursuits, whether you're running Facebook or the mafia.

MAXIM 80

NEVER SUCCUMB TO THE
TEMPTATIONS OF LATIN.

LATIN MANAGED TO SURVIVE for hundreds of years after the fall of Rome because using it makes non-Latin speakers appear that much smarter. "Time flies" is an everyday phrase. Substitute it for "Tempus fugit," which has the same meaning, and to the uninitiated it sounds as though you've tapped into a pipeline of quasi-mystical knowledge extending back to antiquity. The lengthier the Latinate phrase, the more it appears as though, golly gee, you must be quoting profundities from the mouths of long-ago kings and philosophers. However, the use of Latin is risky for the intellectual who wishes to maintain friendly relations with everyone else in the world.

Deploy Latin too often in casual conversation, and others may quickly judge you insufferable. When liberally sprinkled throughout everyday conversation, ancient nuggets of wisdom along the lines of "damnant quod non intelligunt" ("they condemn what they do not understand") or "diem perdidi" ("I have lost a day") have precious little use except as pretentious placeholders—the equivalent of dropping a super-word such as "legerdemain" because that mighty string of syllables makes you seem brilliant, if only in your own mind.

Latin also has an amazing tendency to aggravate those already annoyed. Slip in a phrase like "ecce panis angelorum" ("behold the bread of angels") as you order a bison burger at the local grease shack, and the sullen teen on the other side of the counter is basically guaranteed to spit in your soda. *Sic semper* snooty people.

THEORY INTO PRACTICE

Avoiding the use of Latin is easy enough, no? Just speak English. However, if you're tempted to drop Latin in favor of a different dead language, be forewarned that while Latin can net you a raised eyebrow, uttering a sentence in Coptic, for example, will quickly entangle you in awkwardness over the language involved, the meaning of the phrase, why you learned it, and—no, never mind, we'll just drop the whole thing, okay?

THE INEVITABLE FOOTNOTE

The following groups have a license to deploy Latin at will in conversation:

Latin Teachers: Obvious, right? Otherwise what would they do five days a week, stand there in silence? Come to think of it, high school students might prefer that option.

Lawyers: The legal profession relies on Latin descriptors for any number of procedures: habeas corpus, ad hominum, affidavit, absente reo, lura novit curia, posse comitatus, and so on. Without some of those, how can your counsel bail you out of jail after that little "misunderstanding" involving the goat in the passenger seat of your car?

Public Lecturers: Intellectuals whose job involves sharing ideas with wide audiences will pepper their talks with the occasional Latin phrase. This makes them seem extra-smart, thus justifying the lecture's ticket price, and the use of a dead language links them to a tradition of public oratory.

Archaeologists: Finding ancient ruins requires something more than jamming your finger at a map and saying, "Um, let's try around here." You need ancient texts, frequently in Latin, that describe the location of that palace or city or Temple of Cthulhu. Professors and scholars who study texts from ancient Rome join archaeologists in this category.

9

Walk the Walk

MAXIM 81

KNOW THESE BOOKS.

EVERY FEW YEARS, in a bid to boost readership and set book critics frothing like rabid dogs, a magazine or website will publish a list of the "greatest novels of all time." The books on these lists rarely change, although individual authors sometimes rise or fall a few rankings. The controversy comes when the editors writing the list decide, in the name of argument, to substitute one widely acknowledged masterpiece for a novel of debatably less literary merit. Swap Melville's *Moby Dick* for Peter Benchley's *Jaws*, for example, and the literati will start sharpening their pitchforks for a march on the magazine's offices.

Actually, those intellectuals' default response involves writing highly irate letters to the publication, which only encourages the latter to do the exact same thing next year. Meanwhile, such controversy obscures the main point: lists are arbitrary. No formula can rank James Joyce over Vladimir Nabokov, or Edith Wharton over Jane Austen. The intellectual knows it's most important to try to read *all* those great novels sitting on culture's eye-level shelf. Here's an extremely incomplete list of those must-read texts:

THEORY INTO PRACTICE

Ulysses, by James Joyce: Certainly the book is a catalog of masterful writing technique, with enough puns and allusions and metaphors to keep graduate students picking through pages for the rest of their lives. (It's also a grinding effort to read, and purchasing an annotated version is essential.)

Lolita, by Vladimir Nabokov: Study it for Nabokov's peerless use of language.

The Stranger, by Albert Camus: Absurd, funny, and bitter. Will make you want to sit in a French café and smoke cigarettes.

Democracy, by Joan Didion: The sort of book that makes other authors cry in frustration, the writing's so perfect.

Crime and Punishment, by Fyodor Dostoyevsky: Ax·murderer suffers moral anguish, confesses, and finds himself imprisoned in Siberia: arguably one of the finer accounts of a soul in torment.

One Hundred Years of Solitude, by Gabriel García Márquez: A century in the life of the Buendía family, its key moments shaped by strange and supernatural events. (Márquez is considered one of the foremost practitioners of magic realism, a subgenre that meshes the fantastical and the ordinary.)

Anna Karenina, by Leo Tolstoy: The luckiest of novelists publish one great, for-the-ages work in their lifetime. Tolstoy managed to produce a pair: the epic *War and Peace* and *Anna Karenina*, the story of a tumultuous affair gone wrong.

The House of Mirth, by Edith Wharton: Nobody pierced through a society's bullshit quite like Wharton.

The Great Gatsby, by F. Scott Fitzgerald: Sentence for sentence, one of the heavyweights of world literature. Fitzgerald can imply more in ten words than other authors can cram into an entire book.

Invisible Man, by Ralph Ellison: An African-American man's bitter, funny, and occasionally surrealistic odyssey from the Deep South to Harlem. As mentioned in Maxim 73, it's a pity that Ellison only published one book in his lifetime—but if you're only going to publish one, this is the type of magnum opus you'd want out in the world.

THE INEVITABLE FOOTNOTE

For these (and any other) famous novels, it's okay to acknowledge you've never read them; however, in the name of bulking up your reputation as intellectually curious, make sure to modulate that "No" with a "Not yet, but it's on the list." By deploying this technique, I've managed to avoid reading Jane Austen for years.

CHOOSE YOUR FAVORITE PHILOSOPHER.

IN ANCIENT TIMES, if your goals in life included hanging out with your buddies and working as little as possible, you founded a school of philosophy with the stated aim of discovering the meaning of life. That was probably fun for its first few years, drinking wine and wandering around in the hills, pausing every few weeks to inform some befuddled shepherd that man and woman were once one creature split in two by the spiteful gods. (They had a lot in common with some present-day philosophy students, come to think of it.) Then more people joined your merry little band—*earnest* kids in search of something called *wisdom*—and the jig was officially up: you had to establish a firmer intellectual framework to back those musings.

If the prospect of teaching new disciples the ideal way to exist filled those early sophists with terror, their nerves would have been outright fried by the thought that, a couple thousand years down the road, other thinkers would use their drunken flights of fancy as the building blocks of still more complex philosophical systems.

These later philosophers concerned themselves with not only the best way for people to live but also to rule themselves. Jean-Jacques Rousseau advocated a social contract as the basis of a harmonious culture, while Thomas Hobbes argued that rulers should apply an iron fist to the brutes under their command. René Descartes questioned the external world, Immanuel Kant plunged into the deep thickets of metaphysics, and Friedrich Nietzsche wanted everyone to toughen up a little more.

So many philosophers, so little time. For the intellectual, naming one (or two, if their theories don't collide) as your favorite is positively *de rigueur*: it hints that you've not only read a number of highly abstract and difficult works, but that you absorbed them deeply enough to incorporate their key principles into your life. You live a philosophy every day. It doesn't get more intellectual than that.

THEORY INTO PRACTICE

Choosing a philosophy is a bit like adopting a pet: it looks weird if you select one for a few days, only to decide it's not quite right for you. Here are a few to consider.

Aristotle: This ancient Greek philosopher argued for the primacy of rational thought over animal instincts, and moderation over hedonism. **Ideal for:** Drivers who slow at yellow lights.

Immanuel Kant: In addition to his complex work in metaphysics (you could spend decades parsing his ideas on perception and reality), Kant advocated something called the categorical imperative, or moral principles that are valid under all conditions. **Ideal for:** People who back themselves into intense debates, complete with a lengthy weighing of the pros and cons, concerning which brand of laundry detergent to buy.

Friedrich Nietzsche: My personal favorite, Nietzsche is one of the more misunderstood philosophers, thanks in large part to his infamous "God is dead, and we have killed him." He argued for the shucking of old and hypocritical values, endorsing instead the ideal of the *Übermensch* (broadly interpreted as "super-human"). **Ideal for:** Hardcore marathon runners, social Darwinists, rugged individualists, death-metal guitarists.

Ayn Rand: Few modern philosophers draw as much adoration and anger as Rand, who espoused the virtues of libertarian ideals and *laissez-faire* capitalism. **Ideal for:** Economists, railroad tycoons, Alan Greenspan.

Jean-Paul Sartre: A titan of existential thought, which seeks to focus on objective existence over "essences" or vague spiritualism.

Ideal for: Pragmatists, French citizens, chain smokers, disaffected teenagers.

THE INEVITABLE FOOTNOTE

Philosophers, in their role as champion intellectuals, were masters of debate: they picked apart one another's arguments, lambasted opposing beliefs, and skewered weak assumptions with zeal. In that spirit, should you embrace a particular philosophy, take care to learn the arguments against it: you will almost certainly encounter other intellectuals who embrace an opposing worldview, and find yourself in the midst of settling once and for all arguments that began over a goatskin of wine in the Athenian foothills.

MAXIM 83

WATCH THESE FIVE DIRECTORS.

SOME ARTISTS PAINT, others write, and still more enlist a couple of cameras and a few hundred crew members and set out to film a movie. Considering the immense amounts of time and effort involved in the latter—not to mention the calm and reasonable personalities who have made the film industry so famous—it's impressive that full-length features are ever completed, much less good ones made. Directors of well-crafted movies are conductors of a chaotic symphony, which they somehow manage to build into a moving picture that, if the stars align right, is moving in more ways than one.

Above the ranks of those good directors stand the legends of filmmaking, the *auteurs* whose masterpieces influence pretty much anyone who commits images to film (or "film," in the case of increasingly ubiquitous digital cameras), and ripple from there through the broader culture. Even if you care little for film as a medium, knowing these legends and their works will add to your store of allusions and references, furthering your goal of becoming a true intellectual powerhouse.

THEORY INTO PRACTICE

Orson Welles: When Welles made *Citizen Kane* (1941) at the tender age of 25, he had no idea how much the film (about a newspaper magnate who gains the world but loses his soul in the process) would have on the generations of filmmakers who came after him. *Citizen Kane* so advanced both cinematic technique and storytelling (another director, Jean-Luc Godard, reportedly said of Welles that, "Everyone will always owe him everything.") that it still feels modern today. Welles would continue to push film's boundaries in subsequent projects, most notably *Touch of Evil* (1958), despite Hollywood executives' active attempts to rein him in.

Akira Kurosawa: Another film pioneer, Kurosawa did everything from fracturing narrative in nonlinear ways (*Rashomon*, 1950) to crafting massive battle scenes (including the climax of the much-imitated, never-equaled *Seven Samurai*, 1954) that continue to stand toe-to-toe against the work of any other epic filmmaker.

Alfred Hitchcock: Nobody could cut a film (as in editing) or an unsuspecting victim (as in, every character who runs into Norman Bates's "mother" in *Psycho*) quite like Hitchcock. Suspense and action-film directors continue to play with audiences using techniques he pioneered.

Stanley Kubrick: Never afraid to tackle different subjects, Kubrick over the course of his long career made crime dramas (*The Killing*, 1956), comedies (*Lolita*, 1962, and *Dr. Strangelove*, 1964), an iconic science fiction film (*2001: A Space Odyssey*, 1968), a skin-crawling horror flick (*The Shining*, 1980), and, oh, a couple of war and historical movies. Some film critics (and more than a few cinephiles) would argue he set the bar in each of those genres.

Martin Scorsese: Like Kubrick, Scorsese is a genre-jumper, although he's best known (and most imitated) for tough-guy movies like *Goodfellas* (1990) and *Raging Bull* (1980).

THE INEVITABLE FOOTNOTE

The above list unconscionably excludes the many famed directors worth watching, including Francis Ford Coppola, François Roland Truffaut, Jean-Luc Godard, Wong Kar-Wai, Krzysztof Kieslowski, Fritz Lang, Sam Peckinpah, Sofia Coppola (some apples don't exactly fall far from the tree), David Lean, Charlie Chaplin, Quentin Tarantino, Kathryn Bigelow, Steven Spielberg, and others. George Lucas might have made this list if it hadn't been for that prequel *Star Wars* trilogy.

MAXIM 84

DIVERSIFY YOUR NEWS INTAKE.

BEFORE THE INTERNET, the fastest way to transmit news to readers' eyes involved printing articles on cheap broadsheets and underpaying a little kid to deliver them to your door. Depending on the town you lived in, your information options were usually limited to the local newspaper, a few national ones, and the nightly newscaster. News junkies consumed more: John F. Kennedy kept abreast of ten newspapers, according to his Presidential Library and Museum, despite a government full of wonks whose only job was to tell him the latest.

Then the Internet became a source of news, transmitting those same articles to readers' screens at lightning speed. Combined with the rise of aggregation news websites, which offer dozens of articles from most major subject areas at a glance, your current options have ballooned to hundreds of publications from around the world, thousands of blogs, and millions of Twitter feeds. Your laptop or phone can deluge your mind with the information equivalent of water from a fire hose. The choices are overwhelming.

This is a good thing.

From the intellectual's point of view, online news is a fantastic development, if only because you can now quote from more newspapers and blogs than ever. More information from far-flung sources also means more fodder for debates, more ideas for books and theories, and more feel-good moments when you realize that, no matter how many mistakes you made this week, you're not the little punk who tried to rob a liquor store by throwing a cinderblock against the front window, only to have it bounce off the glass and knock him unconscious. The Internet: eternal archive of the tasteful, the understated, and the classy.

THEORY INTO PRACTICE

Can the traditional newspaper survive the Internet? Nine out of ten newspaper editors respond with an enthusiastic "Yes." The tenth is sitting in his parked car, crying and drinking as he stares at a report showing his publication's latest drop in ad revenue.

Those newspapers with the best chance of enduring the next few years have embraced the online world, offering multimedia and exclusive content through their websites, rendering them that much more valuable to intellectuals looking for their recommended daily allowance of information about the world at large.

The Internet gives you access to more papers than even Kennedy could consume between staring down the Russians and staring at Marilyn Monroe. Reading multiple *Times* and journals prevents your worldview from narrowing to a myopic little dot, filled only with the news you want to see and the expert opinions you already find agreeable.

Individual websites and blogs, on the other hand, present a trickier proposition as news sources. Web-only outlets live and die by the speed at which they can produce new content, as opposed to accuracy. A story posted at noon, based largely on rumor and secondhand sources, could prove erroneous by one in the afternoon. And blogs, which exist mainly as their creator's digital soapbox, offer information with a personal slant. Balanced news is a rare commodity online, making it that much more important to visit a mix of outlets and blogs from all parts of the spectrum. Aggregators such as Google News, Yahoo News, and others help with this, by offering you dozens of headlines and publications gathered in one space.

THE INEVITABLE FOOTNOTE

Trust but verify: unless an online news source comes from a known and trusted brand (a century-old newspaper, say, or a magazine of note), take its articles with the proverbial grain of salt, and compare them with others online. Actually, this applies to the "trusted" brands as well.

MAXIM 85

WITHSTAND THE URGE TO RELY ON PICASSO AS YOUR FALLBACK ARTIST.

IN LIFE AND ART, Pablo Picasso proved an unstoppable force. As a teenager, he was already painting with enormous technical skill. Later he embarked on his rather morose Blue Period, followed by the perkier Rose Period, before leaping into Cubism, surrealism, and abstract expressionism. Ask people to define the Picasso "style," and many will focus on those later periods, when he broke down reality into its fundamental shapes and color.

Given Picasso's outsized influence on modern art, it's often tempting, when faced with an unfamiliar painting from the past hundred years, to utter his name as its creator. This knee-jerk impulse is ingrained in us from a young age: show a classroom of fifth graders a work by Georges Braque or Paul Klee, and thirty little voices will shout "Picasso!" with the passion and certainty of Hemingway saying he wants another drink.

Ask those fifth graders for a favorite painter, and you'll probably hear the same response. But hey, at least they know one artist. It's not like Braque and Klee and Sage and Dali and Miró and Matisse are out there in the ether, weeping with impotent rage as that dark-eyed midget continues to exert his immense pull on the popular consciousness.

Or maybe deep in some famous-artist afterworld they continue to argue, drinking, smoking and swiping paint on canvas and sniping at Picasso behind his back. In which case, do them a favor and cite their names more often. Shouting "Kay Sage" in front of a surrealist painting might prove the wrong answer (and violate Maxim 12: "Know your Monet from your Manet") but it earns points for originality.

THEORY INTO PRACTICE

Picasso serves as many people's fallback artist in lieu of knowing much about art in general. The solution: a deeper education in artists and their most famous works. The twentieth century in particular was a time of rapid artistic change, with movements rising and dying in favor of fresh ones: Cubism, surrealism, Dadaism, pop art (think Andy Warhol's soup cans), abstract expressionism, neo-expressionism, conceptual and installation art, and minimalism were but a few that enjoyed a heyday.

That education means a lot of reading, not to mention whole galleries' worth of paintings and sculpture and drawings to view. If it seems a little overwhelming at first, you're right. That's why graduate students, art-school professors, and museum curators usually opt to specialize in a particular segment of art history, rather than try to wrap their heads around the entirety of humankind's experiments with smearing pigment on flat surfaces.

With enough time and study, you can train yourself to recognize a broad range of artists and their styles by sight. This is a gradual process, the result of visiting art spaces (see Maxim 20: "Follow museums like others follow sports teams"), reading books on artistic movements (perhaps as a happy consequence of Maxim 27: "Buy books by the foot"), and latching onto any nearby intellectuals who enjoy offering talks about their favorite painters and sculptors. You will eventually find artists who seize your imagination, letting you ease off Pablo a little. He never liked clingy types, anyway.

THE INEVITABLE FOOTNOTE

If Picasso's your favorite artist, then by all means use him. The one caveat is that, given his popularity as a "favorite" artist for the masses, citing him might kick off some reflexive assumptions about your depth of art knowledge. If you care what other people think, you may want to add another artist to your short list. "I like Picasso *and* Francis Bacon. They both treated the human form in really brutal ways."

MAXIM 86

LEARN TO IDENTIFY COMPOSERS BY THEIR FIRST FEW NOTES.

THE ABILITY TO IDENTIFY COMPOSERS by their masterworks' first few notes is equivalent to hearing a few lines of poetry or prose and naming the author, or seeing a formula and knowing who discovered it. All are intellectual essentials.

Nearly everyone seems born with the ability to identify the opening of Beethoven's Fifth Symphony. Hum those deep, thudding notes with me now: Bah-bah-bah-BUM. That's a solid start to anyone's music knowledge, yet represents a mere fraction of the classical compositions set to paper. Does the prospect of sitting through hours of symphonies make you drowsy? Plug that caffeine IV drip into a convenient vein, load your music player with the chart-toppers of the powdered-wig era, and prepare for the next stage of your sonic enlightenment.

The same classical compositions that inspired intellectual thinkers for hundreds of years (which is more than enough reason, frankly, to cue them on your playlist) continue to tinkle and boom through our culture today: movie trailers thunder a bit of Verdi's *Messa da Requiem*, in order to add dramatic weight to scenes of an alien invasion (note: not the composer's original intent), and Samuel Barber's *Adagio for Strings* keeps everybody calm in that stalled elevator. Speaking from the intellectual perspective, there are few pleasures greater than needing to hear only a few violin notes before announcing the composer. Not that the knowledge will do squat to help you escape an elevator car jammed between floors four and five.

THEORY INTO PRACTICE

As with books and poetry, accumulating music knowledge is a time-consuming process. Start off with some of the better-known pieces:

The Four Seasons, **Antonio Vivaldi:** This set of violin concertos is a masterpiece of Baroque-era music and almost certainly Vivaldi's most popular work. You've heard selections drifting out of speakers in higher-end stores, on occasion, and overall it remains a stalwart of classical radio.

Adagio for Strings, **Samuel Barber:** Music so soul-wrenchingly sad should come with a full bottle of Prozac. It first premiered in 1938, and has enjoyed a long and popular life since, including on movie soundtracks such as David Lynch's *The Elephant Man*.

Rhapsody in Blue, **George Gershwin:** Merging jazz and classical themes, this iconic composition has endured for almost ninety years thanks to its omnipresence in movies, ads, television shows, and even the Olympic Games.

Ride of the Valkyries, **Richard Wagner:** The introduction to the third act of *Die Walküre*, Wagner's bombastic tune is perhaps most famous to modern audiences as the music blared by Colonel Kilgore's Air Calvary helicopters as they decimate a Vietnamese village in Coppola's *Apocalypse Now*. On a somewhat unrelated note, Wagner was Friedrich Nietzsche's favorite composer.

Also Sprach Zarathustra, **Richard Strauss:** Speaking of Nietzsche and famous movies, this Strauss composition (which drew its name from one of the philosopher's works) found fame as the soundtrack for Kubrick's *2001: A Space Odyssey*.

William Tell Overture, **Gioachino Rossini:** Decades after Gioachino Rossini passed away in 1868, the final part of his *William Tell* opera became the theme song for the Lone Ranger. That might have overshadowed Rossini's reputation as one of the more popular opera composers of his day—but it did help people continue to remember him.

Canon in D Major, Johann Pachelbel: A staple of the classical repertoire so soothing, it could pacify a roomful of screaming babies or rioting prisoners.

THE INEVITABLE FOOTNOTE

Some rock stars, having survived the drugs, booze, and brawls that come with enormous fortune, decide in their middle years to start composing classical scores: earnest, painstakingly crafted pieces that inevitably drive the hardcore fans to demand their idol stick with guitar riffs. Before you give those modern works a listen (sometimes the name on the album is enough to draw you in), make sure you spend ample time with the old masters. And to be fair, whatever the merits of Elvis Costello composing an opera, or Paul McCartney offering albums of orchestral arrangements, the rockers would probably be the first to suggest you listen to the classics before anything else.

TAKE SPEAKING TIPS FROM CHURCHILL.

WINSTON CHURCHILL knew a little something about giving a good speech. "We shall not flag or fail," he thundered before the British House of Commons, after Allied soldiers evacuated mainland Europe in the face of the Nazi *blitzkrieg*. "We shall fight on the beaches, we shall fight on the landing-grounds, we shall fight in the fields and streets, we shall fight in the hills. We shall never surrender."

His speeches rallied a British public bloodied and weary of war. His leadership helped liberate Europe. His rhetoric immortalized him as one of the great politicians of the ages. For those intellectuals who speak in meetings and public forums on a regular basis, the great leader's techniques could prove useful in helping sell ideas to their maximum potential.

THEORY INTO PRACTICE

Rehearse: If at all possible, have a friend or colleague vet your speech beforehand. Take a test run through any visual presentation. Watch how Churchill (or a modern politician, like Barack Obama) uses pauses, hand motions, and tone to emphasize certain points.

Structure: Churchill is a big fan of repetition as a tool for hammering an argument home—observe his use of "we shall" in the speech fragment above. He also organized his speeches to soar toward a major philosophical or political theme, in the same way a story climaxes. These are effective speechmaking techniques.

Focus on Your Listeners: This is the root of that "Picture your audience naked" advice everyone loves to give you before a big speech. By concentrating on the crowd—or simply locking eyes with a single person—you draw your mind away from the sweat soaking the back of your shirt, your thundering heartbeat, and the growing certainty that your fly is unzipped.

Prepare for the Worst: Not every speech runs on rails. A blown microphone, a leaking ceiling, an unnaturally hirsute streaker are just a few of the unexpected events that, at a crucial moment, can leave you at a loss for words. The trick is to maintain your composure. Refuse to leave the stage in the face of a complication, or to succumb to panic: however questionable your audience's ability to recall the details of your speech on nuclear proliferation tomorrow morning, they will almost certainly remember you sprinting around in circles and howling—if you allow that to happen. Once the incident's been handled, proceed as before.

Keep Your Sense of Humor: Churchill was funny. "We have not journeyed across the centuries, across the oceans, across the mountains, across the prairies, because we are made of sugar candy," he told the Canadian Parliament in 1941. Seeding your speeches with jokes can loosen up your listeners. Churchill's humor was often self-deprecating, or meant to encourage his audience. In keeping with his position as a British politician, he had mastered the witty potshot—although he reserved many of these for interviews and dinner-table conversation, as opposed to speeches. It helps to avoid jokes that might offend your audience, like a necrophilia quip at a funeral directors' conference.

THE INEVITABLE FOOTNOTE

Churchill liked a drink or two, although there's some debate over whether he drank nearly as much as myth suggests. Before you subscribe to that myth and take a few shots to dull the prespeech jitters, remember that alcohol and public speaking rarely (if ever) mix well: at best your thinking will muddle. At worst you could take a header off the stage, not exactly a recommended technique for ending a successful performance.

MAXIM 88

FAMILIARIZE YOURSELF WITH THE ANCIENT GREEKS.

LITTLE DID THE ANCIENT GREEKS KNOW their advancements in democracy, theater, and philosophy would someday result in Congress, dozens of soul-sucking Broadway flops, and extremely advanced ways to bullshit. Those unintended consequences aside, the Greeks really did make substantial (some would argue *the* most substantial) contributions to Western civilization, and thus are name-dropped with regularity by intellectuals everywhere.

The Greeks gave us the *Iliad*, a lengthy poem about a fight over a girl that gets way out of hand, and one of the first masterworks in the Western canon. Sophocles, Aeschylus, Aristophanes, and Euripides crafted plays that installed the very foundations of dramatic theater. The Athenian aristocrat Cleisthenes overthrew the tyrant Hippias and introduced representative government in that city. Socrates, the philosophical gadfly, threatened to make people think too much, and so they killed him; he had the last laugh, though, by enduring for centuries afterward through the writings of his follower Plato.

Without the ancient Greeks, modern life might look very different, and perhaps not for the better. Certainly they established much of the groundwork for intellectual thought over the past few millennia, with untold legions of famous thinkers citing the Greeks as the primary influence on their work. For that reason alone, all self-respecting intellectuals should understand something of the people who helped birth the culture they revere.

THEORY INTO PRACTICE

Government: When the Greeks made their first attempts at formulating democratic government, it wasn't exactly a smooth process. The Athenians booted Cleisthenes out of the city for a time. The citizens of other Greek city-states refused to give up their aristocrats and tyrants in favor of rule by the people—or rather, those aristocrats and tyrants refused to step down for them. Nonetheless, the ancient Greeks are still upheld as the founders of representative government.

Philosophy: Before Socrates wandered around Athens probing the Big Questions, philosophers such as Thales, Pythagoras (credited with the famous geometric theorem), and Anaximander did their best to explain the workings of the world. Following Socrates, theorists including Plato, Aristotle, and Epicurus continued the hunt for universal answers.

Art and Literature: The blind poet Homer is credited with authoring both the *Iliad* and the *Odyssey* (although it remains an object of speculation whether he existed in the first place). The aforementioned playwrights puzzled out some guiding principles for tragedy and comedy. Herodotus wrote a definitive history of Greece's wars with Persia. And Greek architecture remains a presence in current times, if only because governments still feel obligated to line their buildings with fancy Doric, Ionic, and Corinthian columns.

War: The Greeks were pioneers in developing methods for warring against their fellow human beings. The Athenians used their navy of triremes (narrow wooden warships powered by rowers) to maneuver along Greece's rocky coast. On land, the Spartans trained their males from infancy to become the ancient-world equivalent of the Terminator, something that paid handsomely when it came time to fend off the massive Persian army.

THE INEVITABLE FOOTNOTE

Some aspects of ancient Greece are probably better left to the experts. For example, learning to read Linear B, the written form of a very early Greek dialect, takes many years of schooling. For most people, buying good translations of a few key texts, along with a selection of books about the period and its people, will more than suffice for an education.

MAXIM 89

MIX THESE HISTORICALLY
FAMOUS DRINKS.

DRINKING AND THINKING don't mix. Knock back a few stiff ones, and the level of discourse will quickly descend from "This so-called 'unequivocal evidence' bears further discussion" to "If you pay me a dollar, I'll try to jump over that Toyota as it speeds toward me." Nonetheless, drinking and intellectualism share a long history, if only because alcohol consumption (sometimes massive) played a key role in so many famous thinkers' public identities. In fact, it can be difficult to picture some of those geniuses *without* a drink firmly in grip, wrestling with a new existential horror.

Whether or not you imbibe (it's certainly okay if you don't), knowing how to mix a few "intellectual" drinks can make you the hit of any gathering, especially if you deliver a witty bit of scholarly history along with that chilled glass.

THEORY INTO PRACTICE

Daiquiri: On a busy street in Havana sits an establishment, El Floridita, which distinguishes itself from Cuba's other dim, smoky drinking holes with a life-size bronze statue of Ernest Hemingway sitting at the marble bar. "Papa" Hemingway loved the daiquiris here, and you don't need to fly to Cuba in order to find out why: a standard recipe (from the International Bartenders Association) is simple to shake together:

1.5 ounces white rum

0.6 ounces fresh lemon or lime juice

0.16 ounces (that's a splash) of Gomme, or simple syrup

Pour all into shaker with ice, shake, and strain into a chilled glass.

Gimlet: Whatever your opinion on the British Royal Navy, they certainly exerted considerable influence on the art of mixing cocktails. Every drink incorporating lime juice seems attached to a story about an imminent British Royal Navy captain or surgeon who invented it in order to fend off scurvy among the sailors. Even if those stories are apocryphal—it certainly would have made cannon practice a lot less accurate and a lot more entertaining—the various twists on the gimlet all have a limey bent: equal portions gin and lime juice mixed with ice, and sometimes a little sugar or an added twist of lime.

Raymond Chandler, arguably the finest writer of mysteries aside from Dashiell Hammett, was particularly fond of gimlets: he had a character in his novel *The Long Goodbye* describe the ideal recipe as "half gin and half Rose's lime juice and nothing else."

Martini: The list of intellectuals who preferred a martini for their evening (or morning) libation is a long and illustrious one: Dorothy Parker, Winston Churchill, Ian Fleming, H.L. Mencken, and many more. Here's the basic recipe for a dry martini, again from the International Bartenders Association:

1.8 ounces gin

0.5 ounces dry vermouth

Pour both into a mixing glass with ice, stir (if you want it colder than a shaken drink), strain into a martini glass, and garnish with lemon peel or olive. You can also substitute gin with vodka.

THE INEVITABLE FOOTNOTE

One historically famous drink you should never try: hemlock. It didn't sit too well with Socrates.

MAXIM 90

ASPIRE TO BE A
WELL-ROUNDED THINKER.

THANKS TO OUR CONSIDERABLE BRAINPOWER and opposable thumbs, human beings are generalists when it comes to surviving on planet Earth. Toss us in any new environment, and we have an unnerving habit of staying alive. We can eat nearly anything, provided you cook it long enough.

Contrast that with a specialist species, such as the panda, which prefer a certain kind of habitat and one or two kinds of food. Generalist species endure situations that would place their specialist brethren on the extinct list. Drop a human being into the Arctic Circle with a knife and a little survival knowledge, and a few months later they might return from the snowy wastes with a moderate case of frostbite and a crude bearskin coat. Leave a koala bear near the North Pole, and the poor beast will be stiff as a hockey puck by dawn.

In a similar way, a well-rounded thinker can survive and prosper where a specialist thinker might not. The master chemist with commercial truck-driving skills and an extensive knowledge of Elizabethan poetry serves a purpose in three very different types of situations, whereas a plain ol' chemist is useful in just one.

THEORY INTO PRACTICE

I don't mean to suggest that specializing in a particular subject somehow puts you at a disadvantage to those who take the generalist approach. We all inevitably focus on what interests us or, in many cases, what proves the most lucrative. But keeping an open mind to new things often leads to greater variety in life. If nothing else, generalists who dabble in many subjects rarely find themselves bored, which is a fate worse than death for many intellectuals.

And who knows? One day you might find yourself in a situation that demands extensive multidisciplinary knowledge, like having to drive a truck loaded with nitroglycerin while reciting old English sonnets into the radio. (Your refusal to settle on a college major until senior year will have finally paid off.) Until then, you can indulge in multiple lines of inquiry for the sheer pleasure of intellectual pursuit.

Back in school, your instructors tried to balance you in exactly this way: a dash of physics, some phys ed, a wee bit of "ethics" in a failed attempt to prevent you from giving authority figures the finger, a few semesters of art, and years of mathematics, language, chemistry, and literature. If you paid attention and did your homework, you probably reached your generalist peak at the tender age of seventeen, equally capable of counting atoms and quoting a few lines of T.S. Eliot. My biology teacher made us learn the names of every bone in the human body. Nowadays, I have trouble remembering the name of the subway stop closest to my house. It's an unending task, keeping our knowledge base alive.

THE INEVITABLE FOOTNOTE

Some professions and branches of knowledge require so much study, they swallow the time needed to dive deep into other subjects. A computer programmer who spends a decade learning his craft, followed by more years building the world's first auction website devoted solely to celebrities' used chewing gum, never had the spare months to learn another language, for example, or the history of Japan's Edo period. This is excusable—provided he uses the resulting millions in stock options to head back to school.

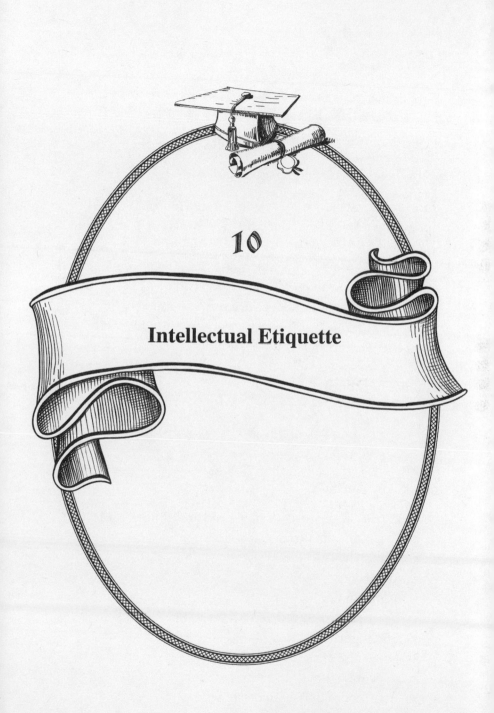

10

Intellectual Etiquette

MAXIM 91

LEARN THE ARTS OF TOOL USE
AND CHANGING TIRES.

SOONER OR LATER, tools come in handy. You might need to fix something minor, like a lock. Or the situation could be more life and death: changing a tire in the middle of nowhere, for example, with no help for miles in either direction. Not exactly the right moment to puzzle over a tire iron or jack.

The ability to manipulate the world around you—and make it work as it should, or just not leak quite so much—represents another type of mental aptitude, as important in its own way as crafting a work of abstract thought or deconstructing a poem to its most fundamental meanings.

THEORY INTO PRACTICE

The first step involves acquiring a suitable set of tools. Useful ones to own include:

- A pair of screwdrivers (flat-head and Phillips-head)
- Pliers in various shapes and sizes
- Hammer
- Wrench
- Wire cutters
- Duct tape, the most versatile material ever invented
- Flashlight
- Small vise grip
- Tape measure
- Assortment of nails and screws

Some fix-it-yourself types feel a toolkit is incomplete without a cordless drill, chisels, box-cutters, and much more. With the above-listed items on hand, however, you can hang pictures, pry loose stuck cabinets, tighten hinges, and mummify a problem in an entire roll of duct tape (among other tasks). Hardware stores also sell ready-made toolkits, neatly ridding you of any excuse for not owning one. Books and websites about home repair offer instructions on every possible fix for your humble abode.

If you decide to build your own toolbox, resist the urge to load it with highly specialized devices you might use once in your life, like a bradawl. Basic tools will suit for nearly all the repairs you need to make in an average year.

In the similar vein, you should own the tools (and a spare) for swapping out a flat tire. Don't know the first thing about removing a hubcap or jacking up a car? Never fear, because lots of people do, and some will be more than happy to share that knowledge. Consider asking an academic: having earned advanced degrees in philosophy, classical Greek literature, or other branches of heavy thought, many of them were subsequently forced to spend years working very hands-on jobs until their first book sold or a teaching position finally opened up. That assistant professor or novelist will not only show you how to deal with that flat, they can probably demonstrate how to hammer out your car's dents and weld some pieces back on.

THE INEVITABLE FOOTNOTE

As much as the typical intellectual believes his or her brain can overcome any obstacle, there comes a point—usually when your entire first floor is soaked in water from a burst pipe, and the roof is on fire—when you should call the professionals (and the fire department) for a little help.

KEEP YOUR HEAD ONLY PARTWAY
IN THE CLOUDS.

THE CLICHÉ OF ABSENT-MINDED INTELLECTUALS, so distracted by airy theory that they risk plunging into an open manhole at any moment, is as old as clichés and intellectuals. In Plato's *Theaetetus*, Socrates defines the philosopher as one "who may without censure appear foolish and good for nothing when he is involved in menial services," without the presence of mind to "know how to pack up his bedding, much less to put the proper sweetening into a sauce or a fawning speech." It bears mentioning here that Socrates neglected to wear shoes for a winter march while serving in the Athenian army, which makes him the gold standard for absent-minded intellectuals.

The Greek gadfly did have a point about his profession; the intellectual whose mind always floats somewhere in the stratosphere causes no end of trouble back on terra firma: pets kicked by accident, microwave dinners over-nuked to a crispy lump, fenders bent, and so on. Loved ones greet these mental lapses with pursed lips, and perhaps one of those theatrical sighs that mean, "If you weren't so important to me, I'd let your distracted ass wander its merry way off the next cliff."

Fortunately for property values and breakable tableware, the truly epic cases of forgetfulness remain few and far between— although nearly everybody, it seems, can recall a distracted teacher who used to quiz them on contents of lectures not given and books never assigned. If that sort of behavior ranks a solid seven on a one-to-ten scale of intellectual absent-mindedness, then most thinkers qualify somewhere in the range of a three or four:

they forget car keys on occasion, or an acquaintance's wedding, but manage to avoid behavior that puts them in contention for the full ten (plowing your Buick through a banana stand because you're ruminating over quantum theory qualifies you for that one).

Constant distraction from the "real world" is part of intellectualism's sticker price: most people in the midst of writing their magnum opus, or studying for that huge exam, have precious little brainpower in reserve for, say, handling the laundry or keeping appointments. Make life easier for everyone: reserve a significant portion of your mental energy for daily concerns. Like your toaster, for instance, with those two slices of whole-wheat bread you placed in it about ten minutes ago. Remember that little event? Good, because while this book swallowed your attention, the toast—more like charcoal, at this point—started to fill your kitchen with smoke.

THEORY INTO PRACTICE

If possible, reserve a specific place and time for intellectual pursuits, outside of which you do your best to engage with reality. Many thinkers follow this pattern, locking themselves away for hours at a stretch, before emerging again with a full mind toward what Socrates termed the "menial services." That mindfulness takes considerable concentration from moment to moment; despite your best efforts, at times you may still find yourself drifting off into the realm of the abstract. Fido might end up stumbled over more than once. But dedicating yourself to remaining in the present moment will prove worth it, and not only in fewer stubbed toes: you'll make everyone around you far happier, and thus more supportive of your intellectual efforts.

THE INEVITABLE FOOTNOTE

Wait, what? Sorry, I was distracted by something else. Did I say something about Plato? Why does it smell like smoke in here?

MAXIM 93

AVOID QUOTING FROM BESTSELLERS.

IT FEELS SOMETIMES as if no corporate presentation is truly complete without a quote from a public intellectual along the lines of Malcolm "Tipping Point" Gladwell or Thomas "Hot, Flat, and Crowded" Friedman, preferably something pithy about how the world really "works." Globalization flattened everything. Snap judgments are best. The only sure sign of a genius is earwax accumulation. I kid on that last one, but insert it in a slideshow and everyone in the meeting will nod along, humming agreement, as if it were a nugget of ages-old wisdom.

Those nonfiction books that purport to explain life, the universe, and everything will occasionally rocket to the top of the bestseller lists and stick there for months, like a wine stain that won't scrub from the carpet. (The secret to such books' longevity on those lists: they make safe and affordable gifts for the not-quite-so-loved ones on your list, like your boss or father-in-law.)

The books win awards, and more people read them by the week, and soon their pearls of easy-to-digest wisdom trickle into PowerPoint files and memos and e-mail signatures across the country. The book's author starts charging tens of thousands of dollars per lecture and, thanks to royalties, can finally afford that beach shack in Aruba.

Then the parodies crop up online. For weeks I enjoyed sending friends the link to the Malcolm Gladwell Book Generator, which created fake titles like *Sizzle: Why Some Ideas Pop While Others Merely Crackle*, or *Yoga: How Hot Trends Make People Buy Books*.

As the (actual) books reach their saturation point, with at least a dozen copies visible per bus or subway car, people will groan loudly at the mention of their titles or authors. This means you can no longer cite those texts without being perceived as a trend-chaser, someone who pulls a theory from *The Tipping Point* because everybody else is doing it. And as you learned in elementary school, "everybody else is doing it" is not a viable excuse for anything. The intellectual aspires to quote from lesser-known works, hinting at a depth of knowledge beyond what you find on the racks of an airport book kiosk.

THEORY INTO PRACTICE

Indeed, referencing lesser-known authors not only boosts your intellectual credentials: it can mark you as a trendsetter. As a bonus, it allows you to avoid any groaning from colleagues when you send the billionth-and-first quarterly memo quoting liberally from the latest pop sociology text. Best of all, those more esoteric sources are easy to find: A quick online search within a selected field—psychology, say, or macroeconomics—will result in a host of books you can use for inspiration.

This maxim also applies to fiction bestsellers: once a novel has perched atop the charts for months, referring to it inevitably makes your own work feel a little derivative. For quite a long time, it seemed practically federal law that everyone tote a copy of Stieg Larsson's novel *The Girl with the Dragon Tattoo*, meaning in turn that every parody and homage of that Swedish thriller seemed old long before the film adaptions hit theaters. Aspire to quote from obscure works.

THE INEVITABLE FOOTNOTE

As with action movies (and so many other elements of popular culture), fiction and nonfiction bestsellers gain added credibility with time: If enough years pass, and people continue to read a particular book, and the author's ideas haven't been soundly debunked by subsequent writers, then you can quote from them without fear of others perceiving you as a follower.

MAXIM 94

REFUSE TO USE YOUR
BIG BRAIN AS A CLUB.

IT SOUNDS CRUEL, but sometimes the world feels stuffed with people whose IQs equal their waist size. They drift into your highway lane without looking or stare with slack-jawed astonishment as you demonstrate for the fiftieth time how to work the office photocopier. They text on their phones while riding bikes at high speed, nearly running you down, or search your two-year-old child for explosives at the airport security gate.

Many intellectuals cope with this endless moron-athon by doing their best to inflict the maximum amount of shame and guilt on the offending party. "You idiot," they growl. "You troglodyte. Do you have any brain cells working in there?"

But using your own brain as a club to smite others is a pointless tactic—unless your goal involves having the target of your ire fantasize about a bike leaving treadmarks across your back. You spent years becoming an intellectual in order to more fully enjoy the pursuit of knowledge and to learn about the world—not to make others feel bad about a perceived lack of intelligence. Use your mental powers for good, not harm.

THEORY INTO PRACTICE

In order to become a full-fledged intellectual, you may visit dozens of museums, read hundreds of books (and thousands of other pieces of literature), engage in endless discussion and debate, develop a couple of eccentricities, memorize some choice quotes, and write a book about how the desperate need for beer gave rise to civilization. In the process you could contribute some new ideas to the collective, and impress that cute scholar haunting your local coffee shop.

It feels like such a waste of that immense knowledge and effort, to repurpose it for crushing someone else's ego to a fine powder. Nor is that crushing always deliberate; in your enthusiasm to share your knowledge with others, you can sometimes end up slamming their intelligence. Take this sample conversation, overheard at a local diner:

Oblivious Intellectual: "Did you ever hear of Karl Jaspers' theory of the axial age?"

Bored Companion: "Who the what?"

Oblivious Intellectual: "This period where you see the simultaneous rise of Buddhism, Confucianism, philosophical inquiry in Greece, and . . ."

Bored Companion: "No. I don't care. If I don't have some coffee in the next two minutes, I'll need to stab myself repeatedly with this toothpick to stay awake."

Oblivious Intellectual: "No, try to understand. I can make this simple for you. I've studied Jaspers, and he has some interesting things to say about how the foundations of society evolved."

Any positive feelings on the bored companion's part imploded at "try to understand." The oblivious intellectual continued to prattle on about the evolution of philosophy, and over his voice you could almost hear the crackle of the listener seething in his seat. I'm sure the philosopher felt like he was doing a favor, sharing that theory, even as he failed to recognize that it had become a sledgehammer swung at his companion's pride.

THE INEVITABLE FOOTNOTE

You can wield your brain like a club against other intellectuals, of course, if they appear willing to engage. That's called having a debate. Just don't make it personal (per Maxim 75: "Fight every idea war honorably and well").

LAUGH AT JOKES MADE AT YOUR EXPENSE.

THE INTELLECTUAL LIFE is a difficult one at times. Galileo realized this when he theorized that our planet revolves around the sun, refuting the Bible, and the Catholic Church sentenced him to house arrest for the rest of his natural life. He was neither the first nor last intellectual jailed for heretical writings, and in some respects he proved lucky: governments and other powers have a longstanding habit of killing thinkers whose ideas threaten the status quo.

Keep that not-so-happy history in mind the next time someone decides to crack a joke about your intellectualism: no matter how badly the words sting, the situation could always prove much, much worse ("The worst is not/ So long as we can say, 'This is the worst,'" as Shakespeare wrote in *King Lear*). Because those jokes are coming—if they haven't started already. Someone saw that volume of poetry under your arm, or noted the way you strung together enormous words into a complex mega-sentence, and decided to take a swipe at what they perceive as your pretension to brilliance.

The insults themselves usually range from the juvenile ("All that book learnin' won't help your face") to the downright nasty ("You focus on that 'life of the mind' crap because you can't get a real job"). Nor are they particularly clever, for the most part, revealing far more about the insecurities of the insult's hurler than its target.

Laugh at them anyway.

THEORY INTO PRACTICE

In 1971, the television host Dick Cavett invited authors Gore Vidal and Norman Mailer onto his late-night talk show. The famously thin-skinned Mailer, already ballistic over Gore comparing him to Charles Manson in an infamous *The New York Review of Books* article, decided to start firing verbal broadsides at everyone onstage. He turned on Cavett, declaring everyone present "intellectually smaller," to which the host replied that his guest would need "two more chairs to contain your giant intellect."

Mailer's snappy retort: "I'll take the two chairs if you will all accept finger bowls."

Say what?

Mailer later declared he meant the comment as ambiguous, in order to deny Cavett the opportunity for another witty jab. But it also serves as a textbook case of how *not* to respond to a joke made at one's intellectual expense. Had Mailer chuckled at Cavett and moved on, it would have blunted the comment's power, by showing that he was self-aware enough to take the joke. Instead he launched into that awkward muddle about finger bowls, in the process creating one of the most uncomfortable-to-watch moments in television history.

Nor do you have the option of throwing a punch in response to an insult, as it can spark some unpleasant legal issues. Moreover, hurled knuckles are the final signifier of your emotions overcoming rationality: a victory for the insulter before your fist rises further than shoulder-level.

Shouting your own insult is a similar nonstarter. Aside from trained professionals (i.e., standup comedians and New York City cab drivers), few people have the ability to piece together a truly memorable comeback in less than three seconds.

So laugh. You could even earn a little respect in return.

THE INEVITABLE FOOTNOTE

If a government or other power tries to ban your work or sentence you to some far-off prison, laughter won't help. In that case, your options include submitting to the Man, or fighting (and perhaps perishing) on principle.

MAXIM 96

STAY CURIOUS.

IN *KILL BILL VOL. 2* (perhaps the most intellectual martial-arts movie ever made, if only because each and every frame seems to reference at least a dozen other movies), the ex-assassin played by Michael Madsen delivers a particular line with world-weary gravitas: "People got a job to do, they tend to live a little bit longer so they can do it." Minutes later, a venomous snake pumps him full of deadly poison, rendering his statement more than a little ironic—but containing a sizable grain of truth, nonetheless.

An intellectual's job involves absorbing information and converting it into new ideas. You need curiosity about the world, or at least certain aspects of it, in order to make the process work. And when you lose that desire to question, it's not a pretty sight: apathetic, depressed, sullen, the mental titan stoops to behaviors that place his self-respect, and perhaps his immortal soul, in mortal peril. I'm talking, of course, about sitting on the couch and watching a combination of reality shows and Steven Seagal flicks (note: not the most intellectual martial-arts movies ever made) until the wee hours.

THEORY INTO PRACTICE

Losing your curiosity—dramatic statement alert—means you begin to die as a thinker. Stuck in a rut, where every day feels like a gray repeat of the one before, the intellectual soon lacks the hunger to learn small things, much less puzzle over something truly enormous. Stress is often the culprit: forced to deal with too many issues throughout the course of a day, the mind does its best imitation of the Alamo, closing itself off from the world.

The best way to break an intellectual rut involves forcing yourself to adopt a new subject or challenge, one outside your routines and comfort zone. You see this happen with artists who embrace a new medium or theme, and in the process reinvigorate their careers.

Stress can be a tougher obstacle to overcome. Exercise, meditation, and relaxation techniques help, along with taking a proactive approach to knocking out the persistent problems in your life. With stress alleviated, you free up brainpower to focus on new things. From that point, it becomes a question of re-engaging your curiosity and seeking out what might interest you.

Maintaining a curious mind takes active effort and a willingness to stay interested in topics no matter how difficult or frustrating. I'm always inspired—schmaltz alert—by those eighty-year-old authors who, instead of spending their golden years nudging their grandchildren with canes and railing about the Good Old Days, decide to research and write an 1800-page magnum opus set in ancient Persia. Old dogs do learn new tricks.

THE INEVITABLE FOOTNOTE

Click a little too far into the wilds of the Internet, and you'll see images and video that will scar you forever. I'm talking bodily functions that should never function in certain ways; displays of idiocy that end with thirteen-year-old skateboarders on fire; and shocking misuse of barnyard animals. You should never stay curious about such things, unless you want to make your therapist very rich.

MAXIM 97

SUPPORT YOUR FRIENDS' ARGUMENTS . . .
TO A POINT.

FROM HIS INNER SANCTUM of high intellectual thought, also known as his unmade bed, Mark Twain once lowered his cigar long enough to offer a most incisive view on friendship, terming it a "holy passion" so "sweet and steady and loyal and enduring in nature that it will last through a whole lifetime, if not asked to lend money."

He had a point there, forgetting only one crucial detail: the rock-solid friendship that survives overenthusiastic borrowing—whether of money, cars, or spouses—can still break under the force of one friend having to defend the other's less-than-airtight arguments.

Imagine you're at a party with your closest compatriot. The night is young, the conversation vigorous, and a debate erupts about, oh, green energy. (Nothing says fun and excitement like weighing the merits of solar panels versus nuclear power.) Your friend, driven by the perverse need to spark some bickering, decides to argue to a roomful of alternative-energy advocates that oil and gas are the way forward for humanity. As in, people should abandon research into renewable power resources, in favor of drilling into every subsurface that might offer a drop of oil—and screw any cute furry animals in the way.

The evening's mood does not improve from there.

Unless you're a sociopath, your first priority in the event of an intellectual blowup is to dampen the flames. At the same time, you have an obligation to back your friend's play. After all, what are comrades for, besides beer money and a car when you need one? No matter how much faith the intellectual places in the abstract and the arcane, you always need a friendly ear (or a useful sidekick) when the not-so-abstract crap hits the fan.

THEORY INTO PRACTICE

"I think my friend has some good points," you tell the crowd. "We might have to consider drilling in new places to meet short-term demands for oil. It might take decades to develop the green energy sources we need."

You add the crucial little word: "But." (I also like "however" and "although.")

Then you deliver the kicker: "I think we need to pay attention to the impact that oil and gas have on our environment, and do our best to mitigate any negative effects."

You have, in a few sentences, executed a textbook example of conversational judo. You have met your obligation to your friend by highlighting some key parts of the drill-everything argument, without undermining your own principles, and (hopefully) helped cool the emotions in the room.

Remember to remain civil, no matter how heated the debate around you. As the Chinese proverb says: "Do not use a hatchet to remove a fly from your friend's forehead." Someday you'll need that friend to defend your own assertions about the economy.

THE INEVITABLE FOOTNOTE

Some arguments, of course, are indefensible. If your friend keeps insisting the world is a tiny grain of sand resting on the back of a turtle, you have zero obligation to support that wild-eyed assertion by arguing for the possible validity of certain cosmological myths. Your best option in this scenario is a joke, hopefully one that tongue-ties the conversation into silence: "Yeah, but if the world's balanced on the back of a turtle, then what's the turtle standing on?"

MAXIM 98

LEARN ONE NEW THING FROM EVERYONE.

IN HIS 2011 MEMOIR, *I'm Feeling Lucky*, former Google employee Douglas Edwards recounted an unusual moment in his first interview with Google cofounder Sergey Brin: "'I'm going to give you five minutes,' he announced. 'When I come back, I want you to explain to me something complicated that I don't already know.'"

Edwards racked his brain and decided on the general theory of marketing as his impromptu lesson topic for Brin, who seemed interested enough to ask questions about things like product differentiation and cost changes. "Later I found out that Sergey did this with everyone he interviewed," he recalled in the book. "An hour wasted with an unqualified candidate wasn't a total loss if he gained insight into something new."

As panic inducing as it might have been for potential employees, Brin's habit doubles as a sound maxim for anyone looking to increase their understanding of the world: take something new, knowledge-wise, from everyone you meet.

THEORY INTO PRACTICE

This shiny new knowledge can take many forms: a creative method of juggling, say, or the finer points of market monetarism. One day, having both those things stored in your memory could prove of equal use. (That day will surely prove a memorable one.)

If you work the type of job that allows you to question people at will—journalists and executives at search-engine companies fall into this category—your chances of learning something new is appropriately high. If you don't, then you could make such questioning one of your intellectual eccentricities.

Whatever your personal scenario, there lurks a considerable drawback: open-ended queries such as, "Tell me something I don't know" tend to freeze most people in their tracks. They will hem and haw, and maybe ask a few questions ("You mean something physical or something mental?") in a desperate attempt to narrow down your request and kick-start their own thinking. They might shake their head, make a frustrated noise, and tell you to ask them again later. Unless they want you to hire them for a job, of course, in which case they will hastily dig up a random factoid from the dusty mental boxes marked School ("I can try to explain the theory of relativity—that was Einstein's, right?").

If you're around anyone for a significant amount of time—and "significant" can mean anything from a two-hour train ride to sharing the same office space for twenty years—they will eventually say something, or display a skill, unfamiliar to you. That offers the best opportunity to step in with your own questions, without spooking them. Wait for the right moment.

THE INEVITABLE FOOTNOTE

Every so often you hear or see something so disturbing, so soul-chilling, that no amount of curiosity will make you want to learn more about it. If you're the squeamish type, for example, a coworker asking, "Want to see something gross I can do with my thumb?" is a prelude to nothing good.

MAXIM 99

ANALYZE IDEAS, NOT PEOPLE.

YOUR INTELLECTUAL POWERS grant you piercing insight into the human condition. With a quick glance you deduce other people's innermost workings, down to their insecurities and kinks. "I think your friend has a major Oedipal complex," you might tell someone. "It's the only way to explain the photos of his mother all over the house. Also, the effigy of his father with a knife through it." You can puzzle out anyone, and use that information to either win their loyalty or prod them mercilessly.

That's what you tell yourself.

Granted, some people are easier to read than others—especially if they happen to be wearing a T-shirt with the words "I Have Major Daddy Issues" printed on the front in bold black type.

But in reality, your snap judgments about others often prove either problematic or totally incorrect. (Your friend's Oedipal pal, for example, could turn out to be nothing of the sort, but an actor rehearsing for the title role in a modern-day revival of Sophocles' *Oedipus at Colonus*.) By engaging in that sketchy brand of armchair psychology, you undermine your credibility as an intellectual who only arrives at conclusions following a period of careful study and contemplation.

THEORY INTO PRACTICE

You can analyze theories on their own merits: they arrive complete and self-contained, open to misinterpretation but ultimately as preserved in their form as an insect in amber. Human beings' personalities, on the other hand, are cagey and subject to drastic change. "I feel my slippery self eluding me, gliding into deeper and darker waters than I care to probe," Humbert Humbert muses near the end of Nabokov's *Lolita*. People you've known for years, with whom you might share a bed, can surprise you at odd moments with an out-of-character gesture, a burst of rage, or a sudden proclamation that they love Lady Gaga.

Moreover, the intellectual who analyzes another person to his or her face runs great risk of offending them.

The Intellectual: "Granted, we've only been talking for fifteen minutes, but I think you're fundamentally insecure, that your one greatest wish in life is to sit on a couch and watch anything that comes on the tube. You've mentioned a couple of books in passing, which makes me think you have dreams of becoming a writer, but nothing I've heard in the course of our discussion convinces me that you have the word power."

Other Person: "I won the National Book Award last year, you inconsiderate jackass."

At least ideas and theories never force you to apologize.

THE INEVITABLE FOOTNOTE

Psychologists and therapists, by virtue of scrutinizing people's psyches for a living, are exempt from this maxim.

MAXIM 100

KNOW WHEN TO SAY NOTHING.

OVER HUNDREDS OF MILLENNIA, the *Homo sapiens* brain has evolved into a unique organ capable of abstract thought. People have come to use that brain, along with their vocal cords and opposable thumbs and senses, to express themselves in progressively complex ways. A hundred thousand years ago, in a cave near modern-day Cape Town, a collective of artists carved stone tools and ground out paint in bowls. Today, we use tiny devices made of silicon and steel and glass to record life around us, edit the footage to reflect an idea in our heads, and broadcast it to the world via wireless signals and fiber-optic cable. We collectively publish thousands of books every year, along with millions of newspaper articles, and post endless ramblings on the Web. And we talk, constantly, sometimes even in our sleep.

That need for constant noise makes silence a very powerful item in the intellectual's conversational toolbox. Wise people talk because they have something worth saying, to paraphrase an old truism, while fools babble out of a need to say something. Or to put it another way: the judicious use of silence gives your all-important words, when they finally come out, an added gravitas.

THEORY INTO PRACTICE

You're locked in negotiations with a landlord over the cost to rent a new one-bedroom apartment. You could haggle. The landlord *expects* you to haggle, to point out the crack in the bathroom mirror or that strange red stain in the bedroom as reasons to knock a few hundred dollars off the monthly payment to his "I'm going to retire in Antigua" fund.

Landlord: "So the price is twelve hundred bucks, heat included."

You: Long silence, with a raised left eyebrow, as you give that stain a significant look.

Landlord: "Okay, a thousand even. And you don't ask nobody in the building about how that blotch got there."

In a more intellectual context, silence is a fantastic way of tactfully informing someone that his or her theory is crap, especially if you want to avoid hours locked in a tedious back-and-forth over a few key points.

Intellectual Opponent: ". . . and in conclusion, I feel that there's no way you can dismiss Hemingway as the best writer of the past century, considering how many other writers spent their careers trying to imitate his style. Sure, he had some misfires. Point me to a writer who didn't. Hemingway's second to Shakespeare, in my book."

You: Long silence, with a raised left eyebrow.

Intellectual Opponent: "Okay, okay, I know it has a few flaws as an idea, but I'm working on it."

The rule of silence proves more far effective for personal conversations than public debates, where both sides are expected to participate with actual words.

Aside from such one-on-ones, silence is often your best option in any new situation, whether a dinner party or a work meeting. Others around you will rush to talk over each other, displaying their ideas for everyone to poke like an overcooked piece of fish. By staying silent, you can take an accurate measure of the room before making your own move, and in the meantime, create an atmosphere around you of the enlightened sage, the one who waits for the right moment to deliver the idea that will prove unassailably correct. Or at least veer the conversation in a more interesting direction.

THE INEVITABLE FOOTNOTE

Some things should always be said out loud. *It should have happened differently. I'm sorry. I love you.* All the rest is worthy of silence.

INDEX